Run to Be Righteous

Reflections on Running and Faith

Susan Merrell

ISBN 979-8-89043-559-0 (paperback)
ISBN 979-8-89043-560-6 (digital)

Christian Faith Publishing
832 Park Avenue
Meadville, PA 16335
www.christianfaithpublishing.com

Printed in the United States of America

Acknowledgements

If there were no race directors, media support, or volunteers, no running race could hope to be successful. So it is with a book. Without input and skilled help, this book would continue to sit in a notebook on a shelf collecting dust. Although each person listed has received personal thanks, public knowledgement is just as important. They are the ones who made this book a reality.

It was Diane who offered encouragement with the initial idea and format style. Kathy and Kari gave honest editing and input, along with asking questions for clarification. Gina and Ellen rescued this primary computer skilled author. "That's easy" or "no big deal" were their responses when putting everything in its needed form for the the publisher. Thanks to Malerie and her skills as a photographer for the book cover body profile. My public library was the go-to place to write, research, and email. And finally, Ariel, Linda, and Chandra at Faith Publishing Company cannot receive enough praise and thanks. They were nothing but encouraging, helpful, and patient with this first-time author. Well done to all!

Introduction

Sports were just a natural part of my growing up. I feel fortunate to have grown up in a generation without computers, mobile phones, social media, and with restricted TV watching. Much of our free time was playing outdoors. My dad—who coached football, track, and basketball—often took my siblings and me to the high school with him on Sunday afternoons. We had free reign of the school, playing on the trampoline, having scooter races down the hallways, shooting baskets, and any other games we could come up with.

Summer involved swimming as Mom took us to the pool several days a week. In high school and college, it was tennis. After a shoulder injury, I went back to cycling and swimming, and it was then when triathlons became the new rage that I began to incorporate running into my workouts. I confess, I disliked running for quite a while, and it never came easy for me. But I began to develop a love for the sport, and it has been a significant part of my life for many decades. It is through the years of experience and studying the Bible in which I began to see many analogies of running compared to life and specifically the Christian life.

A lesser-known book in the Bible named Habakkuk has a verse that served as one of my motivations for writing this devotional book. Verse 2 of chapter 2 says, "Write my answer plainly on tablets, so that a runner can carry the correct message to others" (NLT). I write no new revelation or scripture but stories, insights, and applications. Wherever God has placed us and in whatever activities we are involved in and whatever our circumstances, God can use them in our lives to share the good news of Jesus Christ. It is from this perspective I share not only my experiences but references from the Bible that include others in our marathon of faith, the race set before us by God Himself.

If you already have made a decision to give your allegiance to Jesus Christ as the Lord of your life, may this devotional book be an encouragement. And if you have never placed your trust in Him, I pray God would use this book to convict you to follow Jesus and begin your marathon of life.

1

Meeting the Qualifications

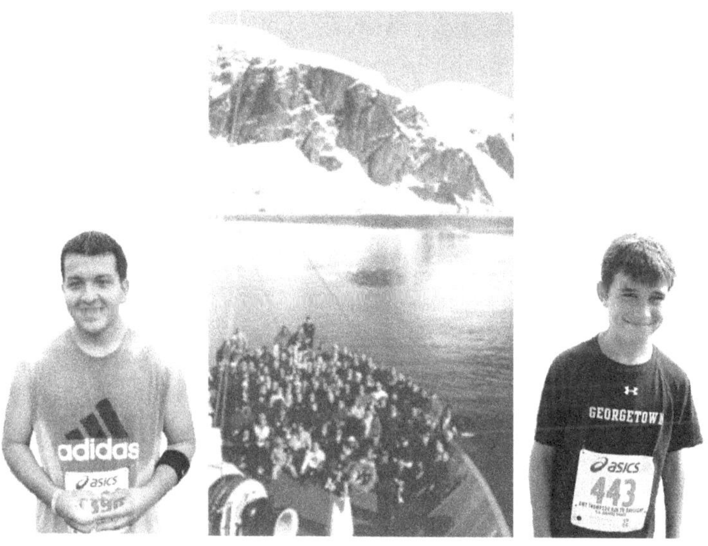

Some people have the misconception that only fast runners are allowed to enter a marathon. This may be true for some races, such as the Boston Marathon and the Olympics. But the majority of marathons are open to anyone who has a desire to tackle the 26.2-mile course. There are no restrictions regarding age, gender, profession, social status, or ethnicity. There is even a category for wheelchairs. In addition to anyone participating, marathons are easily accessible nowadays and available just about anywhere in the world, from the North Pole to Antarctica and everywhere in between. Most major capitals worldwide hold their own marathons.

And are there any restrictions who can become a Christian? Absolutely not! Acts 2:21 answers that question: "Anyone who calls upon the name of the Lord shall be saved." And so, regardless of age, gender, profession, social or economic status, ethnicity, or country, anyone who trusts that Jesus Christ died on the cross for his or her sins and rose from the dead on the third day is welcome into the Christian life. "We are made right with God by placing our faith in Jesus Christ. Again, this is true for everyone who believes, no matter who we are" (Romans 3:22 NLT). Just as a runner is not turned down from entering a marathon, God rejects no one who comes to Him.

Have you ever made a commitment for Jesus Christ? If so, rejoice! If not, please consider the most important decision you will ever make.

2

Entry Form and Waiver

Liability Waiver: I acknowledge that a running/road event is a potentially hazardous activity and I should not enter unless I am medically able and properly trained. I assume the risks of participating in the Eisenhower Marathon, Half-Marathon, 10K, 5K and walk including, but not limited to, falls, contact with other participants, the effects of the weather, traffic on the course, and the conditions of the road, all such risks being known and appreciated by me. Having read this waiver, and knowing these facts and in consideration of your accepting my entry, I, for myself and anyone entitled to act on my behalf, waive and release all governments, event sponsors, volunteers and professionals associated with this event or localities in which segments of events are held from all claims or liabilities of any kind arising out of my participation in this event even though that liability may arise out of negligence or carelessness on the part of the persons named in this waiver. I grant permission for the use of my name and/or likeness relating to my participation in these events and I waive my right to any future compensation to which I may otherwise be entitled as a result of the use of my name or likeness. I affirm that I am 18 years of age or older. I have read this document, and I understand its contents.

PRINT NAME ______________________ DATE ________ SIGNATURE ______________________

Emergency Contact: Name ______________________ Emergency Phone Numbers ______________________

Parent/guardian if under 18 years of age) PRINT NAME ______________________ SIGNATURE ______________________

RACE INFORMATION *mostly flat and fast, all paved course. USATF certified. 2008 Boston Marathon Qualifier*

MARATHON: $500 for 1st overall (both for men and for women)   *(traffic detoured from course)*
          $300 for 2nd overall (both for men and for women)
          $200 for 3rd overall (both for men and for women)
          All marathon finishers medal. Additional 1st, 2nd, 3rd place medals given to both men and women in each age group.
HALF-MARATHON: $150 for 1st overall (both for men and for women)
               $100 for 2nd overall (both for men and for women)
               $75 for 3rd overall (both for men and for women)
          All half-marathon finishers medal. Additional 1st, 2nd, 3rd place medals given to both men and women in each age group.
5K and 10K runners will compete for 1st, 2nd, 3rd place medals (both men and women in each age group).
          All participants receive Eisenhower Marathon ribbons.
AGE GROUPS: 12-19, 20-24, 25-29, 30-34, 35-39, 40-44, 45-49, 50-54, 55-59, 60-64, 65-69, 70+
PACKET PICK-UP AND LATE REGISTRATION: Friday, April 6, from 3-8 p.m. at St. Andrews Parish Hall, 311 S. Buckeye or Race Day after 5:30 a.m. at Parish Hall. Packets include T-shirt, race number, meal tickets and course map.
          Register on line at www.marathonguide.com
Dickinson County Red Cross, 206 N. Broadway, Abilene, Ks 67410, 785-263-2341, 785-479-1626, dkrcorc@sbcglobal.net
          www.eisenhowermarathon.com

All runners are required to fill out an entry form and sign a waiver before they are allowed to run in a marathon. The entry form asks for a runner's personal information, such as age and address, includes all the rules and risks. It often shows a map of the course. By signing the waiver, a runner acknowledges the potential hazards involved and agrees to all the rules set by the race officials. The rules are not to hinder a runner from having fun or running his best but to ensure the protection and fairness for all who are participating.

A similar principle is found in the Christian life. The apostle Paul even uses a running analogy in his second letter to Timothy regarding how to live a godly life. Chapter 2, verse 5 says, "If anyone competes as an athlete, he does not win the prize unless he competes according to the rules" (NASB). This verse is not referring to a person gaining entry into heaven by works but is referring how we are to conduct our lives after salvation. God's commandments and boundaries are not given in the Bible to make our lives miserable but are for our protection and direction. The author of Psalm 119:32 had the correct attitude: "I shall run the way of Your commandments, for You shall enlarge my heart" (NASB).

What are some consequences of not "running" by God's rules?

3

Entry Fee

In addition to filling out an application form and signing a waiver, an entry fee is also required before a runner can become an official participant in a marathon. Over the years, entry fees have become increasingly expensive. One of the most expensive races to date is actually a series of marathons: seven marathons on seven continents in seven days. The price tag is $40,000 (US)! Even a $50 or $100 entry fee may be a sacrifice for some. Many runners, especially in the elite category, have sponsors who pay their entry fee as well as their expenses.

Isn't it wonderful to know that we don't have to worry about paying or working our way into heaven? Jesus Christ paid the price of our "entry fee" into heaven by dying on the cross for our sins and rose from the dead on the third day. Just as all runners, regardless of status, are required to pay the same entry fee, all people are equal in the way they come to Christ. It is a simple acknowledgment of one's sins and giving allegiance to Jesus Christ. Ephesians 2:8–9 states, "God saved you by his grace when you believed. And you can't take credit for this; it is a gift from God. Salvation is not a reward for the good things we have done, so none of us can boast about it" (NASB).

Have you ever wanted to participate in something but did not have the resources to pay, only to find someone willing to pay for you? What was your reaction?

A Runner's Identification

Runners who have filled out their application and paid their entry fee receive what is called a racing bib. This bib has a number along with information about the runner printed on it or embedded within a chip attached to the bib. It is worn on the front of the runner's singlet or shorts for the duration of the race so that spectators, volunteers, and race officials can easily spot the registered runners. Sometimes, a runner may have a friend or pacer run with them. But if they are not an official entrant, their time will not be recorded, even if they completed the entire race and crossed the finish line.

In a similar way, God knows and has identified those who are true followers of Jesus. Second Timothy 2:19 states, "Nevertheless, the firm foundation of God stands sure having this seal: The Lord knows those that are His…" (NASB). Just as an unregistered runner's time won't count, nor will they be listed in the results. People who think they will get to heaven by their good deeds won't be accepted into heaven either. Though it's relatively easy to tell who is a registered runner in a race, it's not so easy to identify a true Christian. One way is to observe another's life, their actions, and responses. For example, Jesus used parables and illustrations in His teachings to help with discernment of false prophets. Matthew 7:15–20 (NLT) records one of these, and Jesus concludes by saying, "Yes, just as you can identify a tree by its fruit, so you can identify people by their actions." But even though we are presented with guidelines of discernment, only God, who knows every heart and motive, truly knows who belong to Him (1 Chronicles 28:9).

Read the parable of the wheat and the weeds (tares) in Matthew 13:24–30.

5

Running Isn't Always Fun

All runners who are serious about their running incorporate some type of interval workout in their training regime. Called by different names—fartlek, tempo runs, and hill workouts—they rarely evoke excitement but more of a sigh or ugh. Their purpose is to produce endurance and build speed. Without it, improvement becomes difficult, if at all. Coaches seem like the bad guy pushing runners to what seems beyond their capability. And when put to the test, the results and benefits of the interval training are seen. And reflection is often, "It wasn't enjoyable, but I am glad I did it."

Training for the Hong Kong Marathon is an example. The website showed it to be a very hilly course and even showed the incline percentages and elevation. The roads surrounding a local lake provided a similar terrain of thirteen miles. Hills to my heart's content! I even named one stretch of road the mother and three daughters. Many times, these were walked. But by the end of my training, I was able to run them, albeit slow. And it was great satisfaction to know my training course was somewhat tougher than the actual race. Did I enjoy the training? No. But discipline and a certain toughness were achieved to help me be successful.

James 1:2–3 tells us, followers of Christ, to "consider it all joy, my brothers and sisters, when you encounter various trials, knowing that the testing of your faith produces endurance" (NASB). This is one of many places in the Bible that talks about the tough times that will come into our lives. God, who may at those times seem like the bad guy coach, allows struggles in our lives to grow our faith in Him. He doesn't leave us so that we go through them alone but is right there with us, encouraging us via another person, a radio program, a sermon, podcast, or His spoken Word (the Holy Bible) and supplying us with the wisdom and strength we need to endure.

Name a trial or tough time in your life that you can say, "I'm a better person for that."

6

The Dreadmill

Absolute boredom is what comes to my mind when the word treadmill is mentioned. Thirty minutes of running on one seems like a marathon. Take away the headset, earbuds, TV, or screens featuring exotic locations and one runs on a machine that takes you nowhere. No matter what the console displays, you are in the same location and with no purpose other than to log some mileage. With the exception of convenience during inclement weather or an aid to the injured, less mobile person, or a cardio test, it's something that will draw groans from even the most disciplined of minds. Who hasn't seen a lightly or never-used treadmill in a thrift store or online for resale with the previous owner having the best of intentions? Dreadmill sounds more appropriate.

Even in its early history called a treadwheel, its purpose was indeed to cause grueling agony with its repetitive nature as it was used by prisons in the UK and briefly in the United States in the early 1800s.

Life, too, can sometimes be boring and certainly sometimes seems to be without purpose; get up, go to work (or school), come home, go to bed, only to repeat the process again and again. The enigmatic book of Ecclesiastes points out the cyclical nature of life, as well as the mundane and often futility of living. It also includes most every human philosophy. But the author, most likely King Solomon, wrote it this way for the very purpose of telling us of what life is like without God: unsatisfying and unfulfilling.

In his lifetime, King Solomon was the wisest and wealthiest man in the world. His net worth would be the equivalent of two trillion dollars in today's economy. Needless to say, he could pursue and have anything he wanted. And he did! His phrases "vanity of vanities, all is vanity" and "there is nothing new under the sun" originated in his treatise of life. And intermittent within the book are reminders that it is God who gives purpose in our lives, and nothing else will give complete or lasting satisfaction. Chapter 3, verse 11 says, "He [God] has planted eternity in the human heart" (NLT). The teacher, as Solomon called himself, makes his conclusion succinctly in chapter 12, verse 13: "The conclusion, when everything has been heard is; fear God and keep His commandments, because this applies to every person" (NASB).

Make time to read Ecclesiastes.

7

The Narrow Way

Isn't it interesting that so many people make fun of and mock how narrow Christianity is in its belief system? And they are correct. Jesus, using an analogy, said, "You can enter God's kingdom only through the narrow gate. The highway to hell is broad and its gate is wide for many who choose that way. But the gateway to life is very narrow and the road is difficult, and only a few ever find it" (Matthew 7:13–14 NLT).

But what is seldom considered is that narrowness isn't confined to Christianity alone. There are several narrow pathways in the sports realm as well. A gymnast has only four inches of width to work with when performing on the balance beam. Hockey and soccer players have their goal area in between two upright poles with a net where scoring takes place. Swimmers must stay in their lanes competing in a pool. Running also has several narrow pathways. Sprinters competing in the 400-meter event must stay in their lanes the entire race. Races that are held on mountainous terrain, such as Pikes Peak, certainly have narrow paths. And getting off the pathway results in negative consequences, disqualification, falling off that balance beam, and heaven forbid, falling off the path on the mountain!

Like the narrow trail or track lane, *continuing* on the narrow path is important in the Christian life. The Bible has several passages using the analogy of paths. King David requested of God in one of his psalms (27:11 NLT), "Lead me along the right path…" The practical book of Proverbs contains many verses related to this concept. Chapter 3, verse 6 states, "Seek his will in all you do and he will show you which path to take." And what a verse to take to heart when God, Himself, says in Psalm 32:8 (NLT), "I will guide you along the best pathway for your life. I will advise you and watch over you."

What ways can you use to stay focused on the right path?

8

Preparation

Airline pilots are not the only ones who use a checklist before embarking on a journey. Serious and seasoned runners have a prerace checklist before every marathon. Some of those items include their packet pickup and running bib, correct clothing, eating regime, duffle bag, racing shoes, and multiple other items. This checklist becomes increasingly refined the more experienced a runner becomes, as well as if a race is run locally or not. For example, I always made sure to have butterscotch discs and a hat. And if the start was cold, I brought an old pair of socks to wear over my hands and discard later when my hands warmed up. I recall making several mistakes when I ran my first international marathon in Paris, France. I could not locate the area (if there was one) where we could leave a bag and pick it up later. But my biggest plunder was how I trained for the race. I tried a training program where I would run one mile, then walk one minute. Oops! There were no mile markers, only kilometer markers. Boy, did I feel like a fool. Many races in the United States are measured by 5K and 10K distances, but mile markers are still posted or called out on the course. Though my mistake was innocent, I had to revamp my strategy.

God has given us a checklist to use when we battle in spiritual warfare. If we apply these guidelines, we won't be defeated and discouraged as we run our spiritual race. Ephesians 6:14–17 (NLT) gives that very checklist we need:

"Stand your ground, putting on the belt of truth and the body armor of God's righteousness. For shoes, put on the peace that comes from the Good News so that you will be fully prepared. In addition to all of these, hold up the shield of faith to stop the fiery arrows of the devil. Put on salvation as your helmet, and take the sword of the Spirit, which is the word of God." And though this spiritual checklist is for every follower of Jesus, how the checklist is used is unique to each individual.

How are you preparing for battles you will face? Memorizing Scripture passages is a great preparation.

9

Runners in the Bible

People have various reasons for running a marathon: for a cause such as breast cancer, for a challenge, like Pikes Peak; to maintain a healthier lifestyle; to go for a personal record (PR); or simply to enjoy the venue or atmosphere, such as Disney World. Did you know, there are no less than fifty "runners" in the Bible? That statement requires further explanation. The verb *run* means to go rapidly or at a pace faster than walking.

Although there are no races or running events in the Bible (other than analogies), a word study of the verb *run* reveals some interesting stories of people in the Bible who did. Their reasons for running are also varied. Abraham ran to greet visitors and ran back to tell his wife and servant to begin preparations for a meal. Then he ran to one of his herds and selected a calf to prepare (Genesis 18:2–7). A young boy went out with Jonathan and ran to catch the arrows that he shot (1 Samuel 20:35–40). Manoah's wife ran quickly (sprinted) back home to her husband, telling him a man of God told her she would become pregnant when she had been unable to have children. They named the son Samson (Judges 13:2–11). In the parable that Jesus taught about the lost son, the father ran to meet his wayward son and welcomed him back home (Luke 15:20). When Jesus was arrested in the garden of Gethsemane, sadly, His disciples deserted Him and ran away. A young man who was there ran naked to escape when the mob tried to grab him (Mark 14:50–52). Peter and John raced to the tomb where Jesus had been buried to verify Mary Magdalene's story that He had risen. In addition, there is a subtle reference to friendly competition when John mentions he outran Peter, reaching the tomb first (John 20:1–4).

All the above examples show a sense of urgency and importance for those who ran. They did so with a purpose. Even though we, twenty-first-century runners, make a choice to run in a particular race, it is also with a sense of purpose. But our lives as Christians should definitely have a sense of purpose and urgency as the apostle Paul states in the epistle of Philippians, chapter 3, verse 14: "I press on to reach the end of the race and receive the heavenly prize for which God, through Jesus Christ is calling me."

Do you know your purpose in life? If so, is it a godly one?

10

Integrity

Another popular athletic endeavor that incorporates running is the triathlon: swim, bike, and run. As its popularity gained momentum in the 1980s, I also got caught up in the craze. In fact, this is where I developed my love for running. I entered one challenging triathlon for its hilly course in the biking and running segments. I trained hard, and my goal was to place in my age division. After finishing, I felt strong and was pleased with my performance. As I was visiting with other finishers, I overheard someone make a comment about lap 3 (final lap) of the bike course. Uh-oh! I realized I had only completed two laps instead of three. Even though I misunderstood the instructions, I was still in the wrong. (This was in the days before course monitoring and chip timing.) I easily could have said nothing and placed in my age group as I was tempted to do, and no one at the time would have known (except God), but my conscience would not allow me to do that. So I told the race director what happened, and a DNF (did not finish) was placed next to my name in the results. I certainly did not like seeing that acronym next to my name, but that was eventually forgotten and certainly lessons were learned.

What if I had never admitted my error? Maybe I would still have that on my conscience. Or what if I was caught in the lie? Maybe a seed of rationalization in other areas of life would have developed. Cheating is just another form of stealing—another's rightful win—in this particular incident. There's even a verse in the Bible that speaks to this very thing. Second Timothy 2:5 says, "And athletes cannot win the prize unless they follow the rules" (NLT).

Have you ever cheated? What did you do? Did you ever make it right? Have you confessed it to the Lord? Has it led to greater sins?

11

One Thing Never Changes

Technology continues to creep into all fabrics of our lives, including the running world. There are multiple GPS gadgets that show our times, mileage, location, heart rate, workout schedule—past, present, and future. The shoe selection can be overwhelming at times with so many choices and frustrating when one's favorite shoe is discontinued. Clothing is lightweight and, thank goodness, breathable, with a wide variety of fabrics, as well as a multitude of styles and colors. Even races are timed using chips and computers, replacing the use of stopwatches. Even how one signs up for a race is totally different than a few decades ago: online.

And while things change in the running world, as well as with our lives and events around us, one thing does *not* change: God. "For I am the Lord. I change not" (Malachi

3:6 KJV). He has always been the same in the past, present, and will be the same in the future. This is one of God's attributes called immutability. He is an eternal God that knows no time barriers and is the stability we need in an ever-changing world.

Name ways and areas in your life that God has given you stability. Thank Him!

12

No Longer a Dirty Word

Tapering is a terminology used by runners in their training regime where workouts lessen in mileage and intensity, and more rest is incorporated. This gives the body time to recover and become ready for race day. Rest used to be a dirty word for runners years back, but research has shown that rest is necessary for recovery. If tapering and rest are not included, a runner is more likely to become susceptible to injury and mental fatigue. The result is often called overtraining. Depending on the runner, there is very little or no running the day before a race.

Rest is needed in our lives, regardless if you are a runner or not. Americans are notorious for cramming in as much possible within a twenty-four-hour period and being proud of it. Some brag about not needing a vacation, while others are proud of the small amount of sleep they get. Even though God never tires, He set a precedent for our lives by resting and ceasing from His creation/work on the seventh day (Genesis 2:2). Our bodies need rest, our minds need rest, and our souls need rest for a time to reflect on God and His blessings in our lives. We need a time of gratefulness. As well, we need rest for our bodies to serve Him with our best.

What are some ways you can reduce busyness in your life, and how will you implement them? Remember to have someone for accountability.

13

Looks Are Deceiving

As the time drew closer for us, eighty-plus runners, to run our marathon on King George Island located in the Antarctic Peninsula, guessing began to take place as to who the winners would be. We had been on the Russian research vessel, Akademik Ioffe, for six days and had an opportunity to get to know each other. My roommate was vivacious, outgoing, and the consummate trail runner, a true adventurer. I, in contrast, was less outspoken with much less running experience. My thin, muscular frame must have given the impression that I could lead the way in any race. Ugh! And a few actually thought I might win, even though I did my best to dissuade them and said that I was a very average runner with virtually zero trail experience. Of course, as it turned out, my roommate not only took first place for the women but also third overall. I, on the other hand, ran my personal worst, having to navigate a rocky, muddy, and icy terrain for the first time.

The Old Testament prophet, Samuel, experienced a similar mistake when God sent him to anoint the next king of Israel. Samuel traveled to Bethlehem, where he visited the house of Jesse and his eight sons. "When they arrived, Samuel took one look at Eliab and thought "Surely this is the Lord's anointed!" But the Lord said to Samuel, "Don't judge by his appearance or height, for I have rejected him. The Lord doesn't see things the way you see them. People judge

by the outward appearance, but the Lord looks at the heart"
(1 Samuel 16:6–7 NLT). And David, the youngest of the
eight, was anointed next king of Israel. He was also called a
man after God's own heart (1 Samuel 13:14 and Acts 13:22)

Have you ever made the mistake of judging a book by
its cover, only to be wrong later?

14

Didn't Plan on This

Many current marathons have plenty of information on websites about their marathon, as well as comment lines on other websites and blogs. It's prudent to prepare properly for the type of marathon you are going to run, such as terrain, climate, time of year, pavement or trails to name a few. Sometimes, regardless of how well one is prepared, some sort of surprise comes up. I've experienced some of those unexpected moments: running an entire race in the rain, dodging taxis on a rather hilly and winding course (that wasn't on the website!), and having to run and walk due to a side ache.

Our lives can also take unexpected turns. It's wise to plan and have hopes and dreams. But what is our reaction to be when things don't go as planned? Proverbs 19:21 (NASB) says, "Many are the plans in a man's heart, But the counsel of the LORD, it will stand." Sometimes we know the reasons for the unexpected; more often we don't. Our response is crucial. The sooner we seek the Lord's help and guidance, the less likely we are to take a wrong direction or succumb to negative emotions, such as bitterness.

Jehoshaphat, one of the kings of Judah, found himself in a much unexpected event—war—and not with just one nation but with no less than three other nations. Jehoshaphat's first response was correct. He sought the Lord for guidance. He prayed to God, acknowledged His power and might, and asked for wisdom (2 Chronicles 20). And then he waited for

God's answer. The same God is ready to help us in our time of need, if only we ask.

Reflect on Ecclesiastes 7:14 and Psalm 7. Prepare for the unexpected by memorizing scripture.

15

A Goal Is Set

As I was arranging plans to visit friends in Paris, they mentioned the marathon held in April every year. Sure! What a great idea, and how fun it would be to run a marathon in a foreign country. There was still plenty of time to train. Though I don't recall the trigger, when I returned home from Paris, I began to mull around the idea of running a marathon on every continent. That seemed doable as well as a great goal and dream, especially since I love international travel. I had no interest in running a marathon in all fifty states, as I knew my body or bank account could not achieve that goal. There are only seven continents, and I already had completed North America and Europe. The goal was set and the year 1997 to begin my quest.

It was also during this time I heard a segment on the radio by Pastor Chuck Swindoll speaking about achieving a dream or goal: "Age has little to do with achievement and nothing to do with commitment." So I set a time frame to complete the other five marathons before I turned fifty. Some of Swindoll's notes on following a dream helped with the motivation throughout the years. First, dreams are personal and specific. Second, dreams are what leaders are made of. Third, one will have a strong desire to fulfill them/it. And lastly, a God-given idea or agenda leads to God-honoring results. I was prepared to do whatever it took to achieve my goal, which would include extra jobs, training, and sacrificing time to name a few. And in July of 2005, I completed my goal of running a marathon on every continent with God's help and grace.

Ezra was a scribe who lived during a difficult time for the exiled Israelites. They were allowed to leave Babylonia and return to the land of Judah after seventy years in captivity. Ezra, too, had a goal, as stated in chapter 7, verse 10 of the book in the Bible named after him. "For Ezra had set (purposed) his heart to study the law of the Lord, and to practice it and to teach His statutes and ordinances in Israel" (NASB). He was able to achieve what he set out to do because the gracious hand of the Lord his God was on him (Ezra 7:6, 9, 28).

Whether short or long term, do you have a God-honoring goal?

16

Alone No More

It was about mile 22 or 23, and I was painfully struggling to finish a marathon. I had tried a new training regime and realized several miles ago how inadequately I was prepared for this race. For a short stretch of the road, there wasn't a water station, no spectators, and *no* runners. Needless to say, the negative thoughts flourished and were coming out of my mouth in weary gasps, such as, "I'll never finish," "this was a dumb mistake," "I'll never run a marathon again." (All that self-talk turned out to be wrong later.) To my surprise and joy, Marsha, one of my running friends, was watching the race on the side of the road. I guess she noticed how pathetic looking I was and asked if she could run with me for a while. "You bet!" Her running alongside me was just what I needed, that extra boost to get me to the finish line. With about a mile to go, I began to see other runners (mainly passing me. Ugh!) and some of the spectators cheering as I approached the finish line. That happened over thirty years ago, but Marsha's help made a lasting impact on me, and I am forever grateful to her for taking the time to run with me.

Every follower of Jesus Christ can also take comfort, knowing that we are never alone in running our marathon of life. Romans 8:38–39 (NASB) says, "For I am convinced that neither death, nor life, nor angels, nor principalities, nor things present, nor things to come, nor powers, nor height, nor depth or any other created thing will be able to separate us from the love of God that is in Christ Jesus our Lord." And even Jesus, in His humanity, reminded His disciples as He told them they would desert Him: "Yet I am not alone because the Father is with me" (John 16:32 NLT).

While visiting his son-in-law, Jethro observed Moses spending an entire day listening to people and settling disputes. Jethro wisely pointed out how this was not good and that Moses was going to wear himself out trying to judge people by himself and gave wise advice regarding how to delegate. In other words, Jethro came along side Moses with support, advice, and encouragement (Exodus 18:1–27). The church, as well as individual Christians, can do the same as Marsha and Jethro when observing others in need of assistance and then come alongside them to assist in making life a little easier (Galatians 6:2).

Reach out to someone today that may need your help and encouragement.

17

Living Water

One of the most important things a runner needs to be concerned with before, during, and after a marathon and especially an ultra endurance race is hydration. (This includes training runs too!) No runner can hope to finish if he or she does not hydrate adequately. Race organizers set up aid stations along the race course, offering water and electrolyte replenishers.

Gabrielle Andersen-Schiess is a startling visual example of the importance of hydration. Ms. Schiess, representing Switzerland, competed in the first women's Olympic marathon in the games held in Los Angeles in August of 1984. High heat and humidity were the conditions for the day. In an interview years later, Ms. Schiess spoke of missing the last water stop. In those days, only so many water stops were allowed. Her body was beginning to shut down in the final six miles of the race. When she did make it into the stadium, her slow stagger to the finish was painful to watch. She said that she was thinking clearly and determined not to quit since, at thirty-nine years old, there would probably not be another Olympic opportunity. With a doctor monitoring her along the way and a crowd cheering her on, she finally reached the finish line twenty minutes after the winner and thirty-seventh out of forty-four participants.

In most races, volunteers help by holding cups of liquid, making it easier for runners to grab. A runner is never forced to drink but is certainly encouraged. Jesus also offers satisfaction to the spiritual thirst we have. He said, "If anyone is thirsty, let him come to Me and drink. The one who believes in Me, as the Scriptures said, 'from his innermost being will flow rivers of living water'" (John 7:37–38 NASB). In addition, the spiritual thirst we experience at the beginning of our salvation should continue through our spiritual life and is maintained daily, just as a runner must continually drink throughout the duration of their race. At the Sermon on the Mount, Jesus said, "Blessed are those who hunger and thirst for righteousness, for they will be satisfied" (Matthew 5:6 NASB).

Are you involved in a Bible study or daily devotion to keep you from becoming spiritually dehydrated?

18

Master Runners

Slower recovery from injuries and slower times are just a couple of the natural occurrences that come with a seasoned and aging runner. There is one small advantage to aging though. The majority of races are divided in age increments. The larger the race, the more opportunities there are for winning. What competitive runner doesn't want a place in their age group! For example, a small a race may only have a winner for fifty and over, while larger races usually have age categories by decades, such as forty, fifty, sixty, and so on. Marathons with tens of thousands of entrants have further breakdowns in age in categories of forty to forty-four, forty-five to forty-nine, etc. Older runners also inspire. Who isn't encouraged by seeing a runner twice their age running the same distance? And, oh, how humbling it is to be passed and beaten in a marathon by an older runner. Master runners can also offer wisdom, including training helps and of course injury dos and don'ts.

In our lives, it is a fact that we all age. In the times and seasons of change and adjustment in our lives, our goal should continue to "run well" in life, as well as being an encourager to the younger generation. Psalm 145:4 says, "One generation shall praise thy works to another, and shall declare thy mighty acts" (KJV). With a more mature outlook on life and godly responses in adversity, older followers of Christ inspire other believers to persevere. Moses did not begin his leading the Israelites out of Egypt and through the wilderness until the age of eighty. Caleb was still a fighting warrior at eighty. The apostle Paul wrote the two books of 1 and 2 Timothy to his child in the faith, Timothy. They are full of instructions, warnings, and encouragements. Aging gracefully is a worthy goal for all believers.

Is there an area of struggle you are dealing with? Ask the Lord to guide you to an older, more mature Christian for help.

19

Paving the Way

"Paving the way" is an idiom used to recognize an individual's work, accomplishment, or mission that enables others to follow that same path in an easier way. In the running world, three marathoners come to mind. Kathrine Switzer was the first woman to officially enter and complete the Boston Marathon in 1967. Lesser-known Bobbi Gibb was denied entry but actually completed Boston the previous year as well as in 1967. Both women had confidence they would complete the course even though society and culture were against them. It was thought that women were not capable of running long distances without severe physical consequences. Because they finished, it paved the way for women to not only run marathons but to take up the sport of long-distance running for health and social benefits.

Abebe Bikila was a virtual unknown (except in his native country of Ethiopia) as he stepped up to the start of the Rome Olympic marathon in 1960, replacing an injured teammate. With 500 meters to go, Bikila passed his Moroccan and New Zealand competitors to not only win the gold medal but to also set a new world record with a time of 2:15.16 and running barefoot to boot! He also won the gold in the next Olympics held in Tokyo four years later. His victory in Rome paved the way for the future dominance of East African runners in the marathon.

There are many who have paved the way in Christianity, the spreading of the gospel of Jesus. Jesus gave His disciples a mandate of making new disciples of all nations, baptizing, and teaching them to observe God's commandments with the promise He would be with them always (Matthew 28:30). The apostle Paul and many of his companions traveled to parts of Asia Minor and Eastern Europe, sharing the good news of Jesus. In the nineteenth century, missionaries—such as William Carey, David Livingstone, and Hudson Taylor— traveled to unreached people groups to pave the way for the gospel of Jesus to be shared.

And presently, in the twenty-first century, there are courageous Christians around the world living in hostile environments. They are paving the way in their countries, communities, and families by enduring persecution because of their allegiance to Jesus Christ.

Read about Christian persecution on websites, such as Open Doors and Voice of the Martyrs.

20

The Great Shepherd

On May 22, 2021, tragedy struck the running community when twenty-one runners died during a mountainous ultramarathon in Gansu Province, China. The deaths were attributed to hypothermia as a result of dropping temperatures, high wind gusts, and hail. Some turned back. Some huddled together in a small hut until help arrived. But six were rescued by a local shepherd. Zhu Keming was grazing his sheep when he took shelter in a cave. (Though no news story mentioned it, I'm sure he sheltered his sheep first before himself.) As the weather worsened, he saw one of the runners and helped him into the cave, where he built a fire for warmth. Four more runners made it to the cave, and then Mr. Zhu saw one more runner and rescued him. This shepherd risked his life and literally saved these six runners' lives.

Shepherds are mentioned throughout the Bible. Abraham, Moses, and David are a few of the more well-known. Sheep are animals that need guidance to keep them from roaming out of the flock and protection from predators. Sheep were not only a source of food and income but were acceptable for sacrificial offerings.

Shepherds and sheep are also used metaphorically throughout the Bible. There is a shepherd mentioned in the New Testament called the Great Shepherd (Hebrews 13:20), Jesus Christ. Though Jesus was not a shepherd by trade, He used Himself as a shepherd and people representing sheep in many of His illustrations. Jesus even called Himself the good shepherd as He would be laying down His life for His sheep (us) by dying on the cross for the sins of those who give their heart and life to Him. We need this shepherd to save us, just as those lost and desperate runners needed to be rescued. Those runners received a physical rescue, but Jesus offers us a spiritual rescue. Isaiah 53:6 (NASB) says, "All of us like sheep have gone astray. Each of us has turned to his own way. But the Lord has caused the iniquity of us all to fall on Him."

Have you been "rescued" by the Great Shepherd?

21

Second-Guessing

Recife, Brazil, was to be my final marathon to complete the seven continents. Sadly, when I reflect back on this race and trip, I have few positive memories. There were very few marathons held in South America in 2005. Normally, I would have waited, except that I had set a time frame to achieve my goal before turning fifty years old, which would be the following year. The roadblocks were numerous for this trip. There was trouble obtaining the proper visa, and I needed to spend more money. There were a number of flight changes, and I wasn't able to book a room for the week until the night before I was to leave! Roadblocks can be either God's way of teaching us not to go ahead *or* Satan's way of hindering us with moving forward. I was not able to clearly discern whether to move forward or not. Difficulties continued during the trip: lost luggage, language barrier, and getting around in general. Race day was no different. My taxi ride didn't show up, and I had trouble finding a ride. Fortunately, as I arrived late, the race also began late. The Internet comments about disorganization held true. At about mile 23 (I estimated), I came to a crossroad with no signs and four choices of directions to take. I realized, my finishing time was not going to be as good as I had hoped. And, yes, I ran down three roads and soon realized they were all wrong. The guy I had been running with decided to quit and hitched a ride. Even though hurting physically, angry, and tired, I was determined to finish. No other runners were in sight, when a man in a car appeared and graciously drove ahead of me, pointing along the right direction toward the finish. I might still be out there lost if it hadn't been for him! Much of the rest of the trip, including traveling to another city, continued with difficulties, including sickness and no phone service.

Should I have waited for another marathon to run in South America? Second-guessing does no one any good. Instead, I needed to realize, the past cannot be changed, and I needed to turn my discouragement and disappointment around and learn from my mistakes. Also reflecting on the positive aspects of the trip helped. God gave me safety traveling alone and help from very kind and gracious people along the way. Most importantly, I was able to finish the marathon and complete my goal. Lastly, I can also learn to laugh about some of the adventures, definitely have some stories to tell, and certainly learned some new dos and don'ts for international travel. Philippians 3:13–14 (NLT) fits this situation well: "Forgetting the past and looking forward to what lies ahead. I press on to reach to the end of the race and receive the heavenly prize for which God, through Christ Jesus, is calling us."

Read Proverbs 3:5–6 and James 1:5–6.

22

Who Gets the Glory?

Yippee! On July 17, 2005, I achieved my goal of running a marathon on every continent. It felt good to finish and have a true sense of satisfaction. One thing I specifically prepared for ahead of time was how and when I would share my achievement with others. Proverbs 27:2 (NLT) is a verse I committed to memory and use when tempted to brag: "Let someone else praise you, not your own mouth—a stranger, not your own lips." It would have been easy to use this to brag and one up on others, especially around those who do not run (or seldom travel outside the United States). I also knew others would achieve the same, newer, and certainly faster goals. In a matter of time and my running the continents would seem trivial, nor was I going to be totally silent about what I did but see it as an opportunity to give credit to the Lord God for allowing me to complete a dream. "Give thanks to the Lord, for he is good! His faithful love endures forever" (Psalm 107:1 NLT). I also took the time to write down names of people I knew that played significant roles: Edna's hospitality in Australia, Fran traveling with me to Egypt, for the opportunities to work multiple part-time jobs, and to those in my church who prayed for me. No one achieves anything great by themselves!

Most of the apostle Paul's letters ended with thanking and giving credit to those who helped him in his ministry and travels, whether it was visiting him in prison, providing food and shelter, giving encouragement, or delivering financial contributions or one of his letters. Not only does thanking others humble us, but it also puts things in perspective regarding our achievements.

Reflect on a goal or achievement you have accomplished and who was instrumental in helping you. Take the time to write them a thank-you note, email, or better yet, thank them face-to-face.

23

It's All about Attitude

It was raining all morning. The only semidry places to stand were under trees or under building eaves. Then, as the national anthem was being sung, the downpour began. A few miles into the race, the rain stopped, but the damage had already been done: feet soaked, sagging wet shorts and shirt (no dri-fit in the 1980s), and blisters formed. I could have complained, become angry, and developed a very negative attitude, but where would that get me? Every runner was experiencing the same circumstance. A proper attitude in difficult and trying circumstances will make the journey more palatable rather than a complaining spirit. I accepted the adversity and made an effort to learn from the experience. Races are seldom canceled due to inclement weather. One lesson learned was to train specifically in adverse conditions. On too many occasions, I opted to either skip the run or use the treadmill (aka the dreadmill). And I was grateful this race was only a 10K.

What is to be the Christian's attitude toward life's adverse trials? First, Ecclesiastes 7:14 (NLT) is a good reminder: "In the day of prosperity be happy, but in the day of adversity consider, God made one as well as the other, so that man may understand there is nothing certain in this life." The Bible is also very clear that life is tough and has its shares of sorrows (John 16:33) as sin and its curses entered the world and human lives (Genesis 3). Sadly, false teaching continues to promise that if one has enough faith or if a set of rules are followed, then wealth and prosperity are practically guaranteed. The apostle Paul is an example of living in the midst of trials galore and wrote in many of his letters about the beatings, lack of food, shelter, and proper clothing, as well as enduring unwarranted criticism from many. On top of that, most of those letters were written from prison.

How can a Christian prepare for adversity? First and foremost is to examine one's life. Is there unconfessed sin? How is your relationship with God? Another preparation is memorizing passages in the Bible related to struggles you are presently going through or will in the future. The Bible is also filled with stories of people so that we may learn from their victories, struggles, and failures. Second Timothy 3:16–17 (NLT) sums it up succinctly: "All scripture is inspired by God and is useful to teach us what is true and to make us realize what is wrong in our lives. It corrects us when we are wrong and teaches us to do right."

Use a concordance or Bible app to look up verses that deal with adversity, trials, and problems.

24

Having Fun

My personality lends to being more seriously minded, nor can I hide my emotions on my face, whether they are contemplative, angry, sad, or filled with humor. There are certainly devastating happenings around the world today. But even Ecclesiastes 3:4 says, "There is a time to cry and a time to laugh." Laughing and having a time of fun is therapeutic and is needed in all our lives.

One of the ways I purpose to incorporate some humor and fun is to name my trail runs. The best experience was running midday and noticing an owl perched on a branch up ahead. With phone in hand, I gradually walked slowly to try and get a picture before it flew off. When I felt I was close enough to get that *National Geographic* photo, I started laughing, knowing this owl was going nowhere. Someone with their own sense of humor had placed a life-size owl on that tree limb. For the rest of the run, I wondered about that breed of owl and if there were any plastic owlets close around!

It's fun to revisit my running journal and read about the Owl Run, the Headless Doll Run, the Ugly Mushroom Run, etc. Another source of humor and fun for running, whether on the trail or on the road, is finding unusual items. This makes for good conversation and contemplation as to how the item got there, such as finding a toy machine gun, an inflatable world globe, or a microscope in a creek bed.

Host a fun run and have everyone take a picture or bring back an unusual find. Or collect money found on your running routes for one year.

25

Greed

After a lengthy period of no running at all due to an injury, the Lord graciously allowed me to begin running again (with doing my part by working on core, strengthening exercises, rest, and cross-training). I was excited to run just one mile nonstop. One day, though, as I was trail running, my thoughts actually drifted toward running another marathon. As the daydreaming continued, I planned a training regime, what marathon I would run, etc. I stopped right then and there and realized my thoughts and desires were greed: wanting more and more, not being content with where I was *now*, and simply being pleased with enjoying what I missed about running.

I had achieved multiple goals and certainly had nothing to prove to others. I am not an elite runner, and my income is not dependent on running. My prayer throughout my time of no running was being able to run again and run healthy. I also realized my priorities and life circumstances were changing, and I could no longer train for a marathon, nor did finances allow for the extras that come with training, entry fees, etc. I also had to be realistic in the fact that my body could no longer endure and recover from the long-distance runs, though I tremendously missed them, as well the discipline that goes with training for a race. I was not content but desiring more, being selfish, and dissatisfied.

Discontentment and wanting more are at the core of greed. We often think it entails money, but greed can encompass any desire. Greed also takes God out of the picture and inserts self. I have since acknowledged my sin of greed and made the choice to simply appreciate the joys that running brings me. Proverbs 30:7–9 (NLT) is an excellent passage of Scripture to memorize when dealing with greed. "O God, I beg two favors from you; let me have them before I die. First, help me never to tell a lie. Second, give me neither poverty nor riches! Give me just enough to satisfy my needs. For if I grow rich, I may deny you and say, 'Who is the Lord?' And if I am too poor, I may steal and thus insult God's holy name"

Is there an area of greed in your life? Why? What is your desire and motivation?

26

Staying Tall

During the 2016 Olympic Games held in Rio de Janeiro, Justin Gatlin had just completed his heat in the 100m and was being interviewed. When asked about his form and technique, his response was simple but thought-provoking: "Stay tall to the end." Running is obviously not a sport where a competitor keeps his head down, especially in the shorter distances that are run on the track. If you take the time to watch elite runners in slow motion, they are upright with a slight forward lean.

This is exactly the attitude we are to have in our lives. Yes, staying tall to the end is important. But standing tall also exudes confidence and a "never give up" mentality. Most of us have felt like quitting or not finishing with our best effort at least a few times in our lives. Working at a dead-end job, a tough time in a marriage, completing a lengthy work or school project, or meeting any type of deadline are just a few of the challenges that come our way to test our resolve to stay tall. Every age group deals with this struggle. Even the elderly can find it difficult though they've had more life experiences to reflect on. Quitting and compromising is often easier than to continue to give our best.

The Christians in the Corinthian church struggled with "finishing tall to the end" in regard to their giving to the poor in the Jerusalem church. The apostle Paul made mention no less than four times in chapter 8 of the second book of Corinthians in regard to a financial gift they promised to give. He reminded them "to finish strong," "excel in this gracious act of giving," and "to finish what you started a year ago." He even mentions the fact how other churches had also given so that the Corinthians would have an example to follow. Paul also encouraged other Christians during his visits, and those encouraging words are applicable to us today, followers of Jesus Christ: "So let's not get tired of doing what is good. At just the right time, we will reap a harvest of blessing if we don't give up" (Galatians 6:9 NLT).

Are there any areas in your life where you are struggling to stay tall to the end?

27

The Right Direction

It is a race director's nightmare, but unfortunately, sometimes a runner makes a turn going the wrong direction. This very thing happened with the lead runners during the 2017 Venice Marathon. Either the course is poorly marked, a volunteer points toward the wrong direction, or a crucial sign or marker doesn't get put in its proper location. Ideally, there is someone on the course to redirect, or the runner realizes their mistake and backtracks.

Jonah was a man who knew exactly what direction he was to go in his life. God sent him on a mission to Nineveh to share about the need for the people to repent of their sins and turn to the true and living God. Prejudice against people isn't just a modern problem. The Ninevites were feared and despised for their cruelty and pagan worship. So it wasn't by accident that Jonah purposely "ran" in the opposite direction. He boarded a ship sailing westbound instead of eastbound in the direction of Nineveh. As a result of his disobedience, he was thrown off the ship during a storm and swallowed by a massive fish. God mercifully allowed Jonah to live, and he wisely changed his mind and obeyed God. As a result, an entire city came to believe the true God.

Are you purposely going in the wrong direction morally, financially, or spiritually? Turn around now, ask for God's forgiveness, and allow Him to get you back on track.

28

In Honor Of

A question that I'm frequently asked regarding my running is, "What was your favorite marathon?" It is not a favorite per se, but the one that has personally meant the most to me was the Bataan Death March Memorial Marathon held at White Sands Military Base in La Cruces, New Mexico. Two other friends and I ran this marathon in 2009. What made it special was running in honor of two US soldiers, Billy D. Templeton and Jack T. Woodson, survivors of the torturous eighty-mile journey that took place beginning April 9, 1942 at the hands of the Japanese military. Not only did these two men survive the death march but also the brutality in POW camps and as work slaves in Japan. Mr. Templeton wrote of his experiences in a book entitled *Manila Bay Sunset: The Long March into Hell.* We interviewed both before and after the marathon and listened to their stories. What a privilege it was to get to know these men for a short time as both would die within the next couple of years. Many years of their lives were sacrificed to ensure the freedom we have now as United States citizens.

In 2 Samuel 1:17–27, David, who was soon to be king, wrote a song to honor King Saul and his friend Jonathan of their death. He also honored the mighty heroes who had fallen. King David again gives tribute to his mighty warriors by listing their names in 1 Chronicles 11–12.

Take the time to interview a veteran.

29

Good News

Before email, snail mail, and even the Pony Express, messages were delivered via a runner. Runners were often used in ancient times for relaying messages, especially during wartime and between leaders of countries. The most well-known example of this in the running community is the story of Pheidippides. Though there are variations of this story, he was thought to be the messenger that carried the news across the plain of Marathon to Athens, relaying the military victory (Nike) of the Greek's defeat over the Persians. Messengers are also mentioned throughout the Bible, some delivering good news and some bad news. Absalom had sent messengers throughout Jerusalem to stir up rebellion. King David received a message that Israel had joined his son Absalom in a conspiracy against him (2 Samuel 15:10, 13). King David sent messengers to Abigail to ask her to become his wife (1 Samuel 25:39). There are even messengers in the spirit world (2 Corinthians 12:7).

Even though Pheidippides or those messengers mentioned in the Bible delivered important news, this doesn't compare to the women who relayed the most important message to date, that Jesus Christ rose from the dead. Mary Magdalene and other women expecting to find Jesus's body on that very early morning were greeted by an angel (also a messenger) who told them Jesus had risen from the dead and to relay that message to the disciples. Matthew 28:8–9 says,

"The women ran quickly from the tomb." That is a message worthy of running!

When was the last time you shared the good news of Jesus Christ?

30

Wa...Wa...Wa

Completing a marathon brings relief, joy, pain (though short-lived most of the time), as well as a sense of accomplishment. I'm unable to recall which marathon, but afterward, as finishers were gathering around, eating, celebrating, and visiting, I couldn't help but overhear one man and his incessant complaining: The course was lousy and not well marked; there were not enough water stops; organization could have been better; there was not enough food choices afterward; the entry fee was too high; the weather wasn't what was forecasted.

On and on he whined. I found myself quickly exiting the area as I didn't want to be caught having to personally listen to him. A cure I found for this—in the running community anyway—was to volunteer at one race for every race I participated in. It gave me a greater appreciation for those who organizes races. Packet pickup, course monitoring, handing out water, collecting trash are just a few examples of jobs needed. There would be no races if there were no volunteers.

The same principle carries over into our daily lives. The Israelites spent forty years in the wilderness and complaining much of that time. God always supplied their needs. But God also severely disciplined them when they whined and murmured, until eventually those who originally left Egypt were not allowed to enter the Promise Land. They were a very ungrateful lot. How grateful are you? Do you have the reputation of being a complainer or a thankful person?

Read Numbers 14.

31

Runners Are Ordinary People

A friend of mine was entering his first 5K. He and I stood toward the back of the pack. And while waiting for the gun signal to begin the race, one of his comments made me smile: "These runners are just ordinary people."

"Well, what did you expect?" I asked.

He was expecting lean, mean people speaking some foreign running language. He was impressed how friendly and upbeat everyone was and some just as nervous. He wasn't alone in his misconception that people who run are fast and in the peak of health. Many begin running *to* get in shape as well as for a multitude of other reasons.

People may also have similar misconceptions of Christians. Followers of Jesus come from all walks of life, economic and social backgrounds, and from many nations. Christians are ordinary people, just different on the inside. And though most runners are ordinary, some have gone on to do extraordinary things. Likewise, the Bible is full of stories of ordinary people whom God chose to accomplish His will. A servant girl, whose name is never given, was instrumental in the connection of Naaman to Elijah via Naaman's wife. It brought about Naaman's healing from leprosy (2 Kings 5:1–19). David was a shepherd, poet, and musician before becoming a king of Israel. Matthew was a despised tax collector before being selected by Jesus to become one of His disciples. He eventually wrote one of the gospel books that is part of the Bible. And Dorcas was a seamstress of no worldly importance but was raised from the dead by the apostle Peter, which was a catalyst to further spread Christianity in that region (Acts 9:32–42).

Ask the Lord to use you to doing something extraordinary in His kingdom.

32

Light

A favorite race of mine is a 5K called Night Flight, an appropriate title as it is held after sunset, usually in June. For several years, the course was on the road with a couple of challenging hills but well lit by the streetlights. Then course changes were made, resulting in a few places along the new route that were not as brightly lit, even though there were plenty of volunteers, spectators, and security to ensure each runner's safety. Running at night does call for a heightened awareness and a slightly different focus, such as looking down more often. Without lighting along any route, a runner's pace would definitely slow down, maybe to even a walk. Falling would be likely, if not inevitable. Ultradistance runners who run at night use flashlights or headlamps. We need light to see where we are going.

The Bible speaks much about light. In fact, God, who is light (1 John 1:5), said, "Let there be light," when He began His creation work (Genesis 1:3). The writer of Psalm 119 uses light to describe God's word, lighting our way in life in verse 105. Christians are "to let our light shine before men that they may see our good works and glorify our Father who is in heaven" (Matthew 5:16). And Jesus, speaking to a crowd, said, "I am the light of the world. If you follow me you won't have to walk in darkness because you will have the light that leads to life" (John 8:12).

How are you letting your light shine before men?

33

Admiration

I admire two well-known athletes. One is Eric Liddell, a world-class sprinter and Olympic champion. The other is Byron Nelson, a professional golfer in the 1930s and '40s. The primary reason for my admiration is that both these men left their sport at the peak of their careers. Few athletes are known for that sacrifice.

Eric Liddell grew up in the northern region of China in a missionary family and said, throughout his life, he would return to China, continuing to serve in that capacity. After a phenomenal running career as a collegiate and Olympian, he made good on his word after winning several medals in the 1924 Olympics in Paris. He returned to China and even died there serving as a missionary.

Even though Byron Nelson was not a runner, he was at the top of his sport in his day and still holds the record for winning eleven consecutive tournaments and a total of eighteen PGA wins in 1945. At the age of thirty-four, he, too, made good on his word to retire as a professional golfer when he earned enough money to purchase a ranch.

Two characteristics stand out about these men. First, they had long-term goals and didn't allow the world's lure of fame and fortune to get in the way of that. First John 1:15 speaks of this very thing: "Do not love this world, nor the things it offers you. For when you love the world, you do not have the love of the Father" (NLT). Second, both were

Christians and maintained their integrity their entire lives. They had the solid foundation that Jesus spoke about and used as an illustration. The wise man who followed Christ built his house on solid rock, and the foolish man, who went his own way, built his house on sand. The house on the rock survived the storms and floodwaters, but the other collapsed (Matthew 7:24–29). God allowed both Mr. Liddell and Mr. Nelson to continue being active in their sports, albeit in a different capacity, throughout their lives as they served others.

In the book named after him, read chapter 1 about Daniel, how he stood firm in his faith and commitment, and how he was honored by both God and people his entire lifetime.

34

Let Us...

Running in a large marathon along with thousands is thrilling. Being around so many like-minded people is inspiring and motivating. And running a marathon in a country other than your own is even more exciting. There is this unspoken sense of camaraderie even if you don't understand every language that runners are speaking. Everyone present has worked hard and has the same goal: to do his or her best and cross the finish line. A marathon is a condensed version how Christianity should be lived out: a community of like-minded individuals moving forward together.

There is a phrase in the Bible (mainly in the New Testament) that talks of that like-mindedness, "let us." It is found no less than twenty times, and many of those verses are in the book of Hebrews. Even an analogy of running contains this phrase: "*Let us* lay aside every weight and the sin which so easily entangles us and *let us* run with endurance the race set before us" (Hebrews 12:1). Hebrews 4:14 says, "*Let us* hold firmly to what we believe." Other verses say *let us* sing for joy and *let us* come before His presence with thanksgiving (Psalm 95:6), as well as *let us* love one another found in 1 John 4:7. Even though we Christians have the responsibility of running our own race (living our lives responsibly), we also have an obligation toward our brothers and sisters in Christ. These examples of "*let us*" serve as guidelines to promote unity as we strive toward the finish line.

How is your relationship with fellow believers? Do you need to make amends with someone, forgive another, or receive forgiveness? Is there a sense of unity in your church?

35

Pain

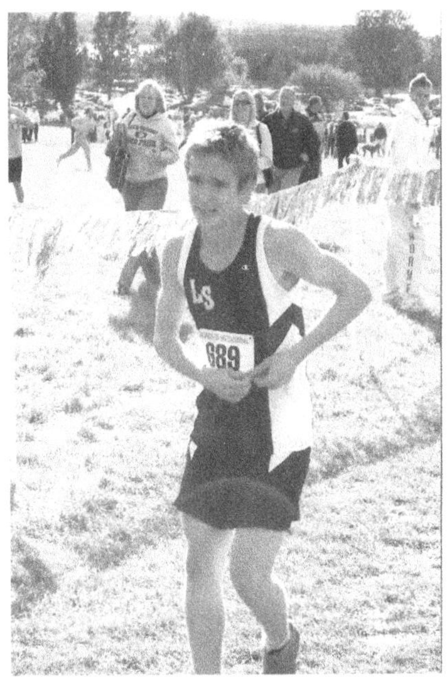

Pain!—what runner hasn't experienced it at one time or another, whether it's during a race, a training session, or a result of an injury incurred. No one I know likes or enjoys pain. And what exactly is pain, and what is its purpose? It's a signal from our bodies, telling us something is wrong and needs attention, like the check engine light on your car dashboard. Immediate attention can prevent further injury. How a runner deals with pain is the key for healing. If it occurs during a race, it may be possible to run with it, hoping to finish. Some, though, have chronic pain, knowing full well the reason for it but refuse to deal with it, make excuses, mask it with medication, or hoping it just goes away.

There's another kind of pain just as real and hurtful, and this is emotional pain. This type of pain may come from negative emotions that haven't been dealt with, such as depression, anger, sorrow, and bitterness to name a few. Pain can be the result of uncontrollable events that occur in all our lives. The same holds true for this pain, as well as the physical type: It needs immediate attention. Jesus Christ endured physical and emotional pain also. God truly cares for His children and the pains we go through. First Peter 5:7 (NLT) supports this: "Give all your worries and cares to God for He cares about you." And another comforting verse is found in Psalm 147:3 (NASB): "He heals the brokenhearted and binds up their wounds."

Read Isaiah 53 and Hebrews 4:14–16 how Jesus relates to our pain.

<h1 style="text-align:center">36</h1>

✦❖✦

Pacing

One of the unspoken rules of etiquette at any race happens at the start where runners place themselves. Elite and fast runners move to the front, while slower runners place themselves behind. The slower the runner, the farther back he stands. How does a runner know where to stand? One needs to know his pace, a consistent and steady motion. In larger races, there are pacers with placards showing the pace they will be running. For those new to marathon running, keeping your pacer in sight is an encouragement to persevere and to remain steady throughout the entire race. Some elite runners in marathons have pacers called rabbits, which will run with them for some of the distance. Pacing prevents a runner from going out too fast or lagging behind. Seasoned runners usually know their pace, and oftentimes runners will run with someone else or with a group. Losing focus and running too fast may give a false sense of security as other competitors are being passed, until body fatigue sets in too early. Lagging behind and being passed is very discouraging. Quitting is tempting.

In our lives, we also want to pace ourselves. It's not healthy to be so busy and live life in sprint mode. Neither is it wise to be lazy or complacent. In the Bible, the four gospels—Matthew, Mark, Luke, and John—recount the life of Jesus. Each book is unique in its account. Reading Mark gives one a sense of Jesus on the go, constantly teaching and healing (check out how many times the word immediately is used). But on a number of occasions in the book of John, Jesus seems to take too long when meeting a requested need, such as arriving in Bethany *after* his friend Lazarus died (John 11:21). But reading all accounts, one notices that even though Jesus was constantly on the move, constantly interrupted, constantly challenged, and always had people following him, he was never in a hurry. There's no mention of him running because he was late or even that he needed a vacation. He took time to rest, get away, pray (Luke 5:16), build relationships, while at the same time having a perfect focus of His purpose here on earth. He knew exactly how to pace Himself.

Read the account of Jesus being "late" in John 11.

37

Stumbling

Whether during the Olympics or World Championships, the 10,000-meter race seldom disappoints spectators. What makes this race exciting is the close proximity the runners are to each other: shoulder to shoulder. Though it doesn't happen often, stumbling shouldn't be a surprise when a dozen or so competitors are running fast and within inches of each other. Strategy also plays a factor as the expected winner is often boxed in and, with a fast pace, has difficulty breaking free to make a move. Two world-class runners, Lasse Virén and Mo Farah, have experienced stumbling in their careers. Viren was competing in the Summer Olympic Games in 1972, which were held in Munich, Germany. Legs were entangled, and two runners went down. Viren got up and ran until he caught up with the pack. He then distanced himself in the last 100 meters or so, winning the gold medal in spectacular fashion. At the 2017 World Championships held in London, Mo Farah didn't fall to the ground, but he stumbled in the pack during the bell lap and also recovered to win with distance between him and the rest of the group. Their wins are inspiring.

The prophet Micah told his enemies, "Do not gloat over me, my enemies! For though I fall, I will rise again. Though I sit in darkness the Lord will be my light" (Micah 7:8 NLT). Proverbs 24:16 says, "The godly may trip seven times, but they will get up again." Lasse Virén could have stayed there on the track, feeling like a failure, but he chose to get up and keep going. Christians also have a responsibility to not cause others to stumble, as mentioned in Romans 14:13, 1 Corinthians 8:9, and 1 John 2:10. And even though very difficult, we are not even to gloat over our enemies when *they* stumble (Proverbs 24:17)!

Read Psalm 37:24, 66:9, and 121:3.

38

Beauty at the Races

Beautiful people don't come to mind when visualizing marathon runners. Good-hearted people along the race course often yell out, "Looking good," while every runner knows and often wants to yell back, "No, I don't," or "You're blind!" I don't know too many competitors that look great at mile 24 during a hot and humid marathon or at the end of a brutal ultratrail race. There was one runner known who did personify beauty during competition, and that was Florence Griffith Joyner, Olympic winner and world record holder in the 100m and 200m. She didn't leave looks at the door as she often sported her own bold fashion designs on the track, as well as her signature long painted fingernails. Many runners, though, do get caught up in the looks aspect of the sport. And athletic sportswear companies cater well to that "got to have it" mentality. It's one thing to purchase the best gear for weather, durability, and comfort; it's another to solely focus on looking good while running. If runners don't train or run well, all the latest fashion won't make them a better runner.

Christians are commanded to take care of our bodies since the Holy Spirit resides in us. "Don't you realize that your body is the temple of the Holy Spirit, who lives in you and was given to you by God? You do not belong to yourself, for God bought you with a high price. So you must honor God with your body" (1 Corinthians 6:19–20 NLT). There was a group of religious leaders in biblical times called the

Pharisees. Sadly, their outward appearance did not match their inward selves. Jesus confronted them on many counts regarding their hypocrisy. "What sorrow awaits you teachers of religious law and you Pharisees. Hypocrites! For you are whitewashed tombs – beautiful on the outside but filled on the inside with dead people's bones and all sorts of impurity. Outwardly you look like righteous people, but inwardly your hearts are filled with hypocrisy and lawlessness" (Matthew 23:27–28 NLT). That scathing rebuke should be a reminder to us Christians to "clothe ourselves with a heart of compassion, kindness, humility, gentleness and patience" (Colossians 3:12).

Are there any inward sins that need addressing, such as lying, gossiping, or cheating?

39

Beautiful Feet

The feet play a significant role in a runner's performance. Without properly fitting shoes, blisters can quickly form. Those who do run barefoot know the ground can be a source of numerous unwanted objects that impede running. Calluses, blood blisters, blackened, and missing toenails are a few of the casualties experienced by seasoned competitors. One thing runners are not known for and that is beautiful feet. A long-time runner has feet that have a similar look of a person who has worked with their hands all their life: worn.

But the Bible describes "how beautiful on the mountains are the feet of the messenger who brings good news, the good news of peace and salvation, the news that the God of Israel reigns" (Isaiah 52:7 NLT)! And those beautiful feet are still sharing the good news today, whether the messenger is wearing sandals, running shoes, high heels, or even barefoot. And no feet are more beautiful than those of Jesus Christ, whose hands and feet were nailed to a cross (Luke 24:39–40). And Christians will someday be able to see those scars as they serve as an eternal reminder of His death and resurrection for the salvation from our sins.

Pray for opportunity to share the good news.

40

Cheering

What athletes competing in their sport don't want a home crowd cheering them on to victory? Team sports, such as football, basketball, and soccer are most commonly thought of when it comes to spectators. But even running has just as enthusiastic fans, from the Olympics to a junior high cross-country meet. If a marathon is not located in a convenient or populated area, the start and finish always have people present, cheering on runners. Even the marathon in Antarctica had a few men come out from their research stations for a while to cheer us on. What a feeling it must be when the front runner in the Olympic marathon first enters the stadium to tens of thousands cheering. The runner can't help but be motivated to continue strong and even sprint to the end on that final lap.

Hebrews 12:1 seems to present a similar analogy as it mentions, "Therefore since we are surrounded by so great a cloud of witnesses…" We can certainly envision people in heaven looking down on us as we run our Christian marathon. But the "so great a cloud of witnesses" actually refers to those mentioned in the hall of faith listed in the previous chapter, as well as those who have followed them. Their lives are to be studied as an example as to how we are to run, persevere, and not give up before finishing the race God has set before each of us as followers of Christ.

Is there anyone you know that exemplifies living by faith? Thank them. Are you cheering someone on to remain faithful?

41

Sexual Purity

When thinking about running in a race or even running for the love of it, forward motion is what is visualized, not running away. But there are times when it is necessary to run away, while other times it is not the right thing to do, such as *running* from responsibility.

The Bible mentions stories of those who did run away, and their reasons vary. Hagar was being mistreated by Sarai and ran away (Genesis 16:6). David was seemingly always on the run from King Saul, who, in fits of jealousy and rage, wanted him dead and continually tried to hunt him down. How do you think Jesus felt (even though He knew ahead of time) when His disciples ran away and abandoned Him in the garden of Gethsemane (Matthew 26:56, Mark 14:50)?

There is always a time to run away when it comes to sexual temptations. First Corinthians 6:18 (NLT) says, "Run from sexual sin! No other sin so clearly affects the body as this one does. For sexual immorality is a sin against your own body." Joseph, and his story, is an excellent example to learn from. He was in charge of Potiphar's household and all that he owned. But Potiphar's wife had an eye for Joseph, who was handsome and well-built. She constantly pressured him to have sex with her, and he would do his best to avoid her. But one day, she literally grabbed him, demanding him to sleep with her, and he took off, leaving his cloak behind. Sexual purity in this day and age is laughed at and thought of as old thinking. But God, the Creator of us and sex, has provided boundaries for human sexuality (Mark 10:5–9). And when sexual temptations do come into our lives, God will help. "The temptations in your life are no different from what others experience. And God is faithful. He will not allow the temptation to be more than you can stand. When you are tempted, He will show you a way out so that you can endure" (1 Corinthians 10:13 NLT).

If you are a follower of Jesus Christ, are you following God's standard for sexual purity? Also, read Genesis 2:21–25 and 1 Corinthians 7:1–9.

42

Rough Terrain

The rocky beach, the muddy service roads, and crunchy ice on King George Island; the sand pit at White Sands Missile Base; uncovered tree roots on the trails at Wallace State Park; the unknown holes on a bad cross-country course; and the blistering hot pavement on many a summer race—these are some of the rough terrains of races I've run. Isn't it interesting that when recalling races, it's the toughest and most difficult that we best remember, how we endured, didn't quit, and what strategies we used or the ones we should have! Those terrains reveal our character as a runner, as well as how appropriately we trained. Knowing the terrain ahead of time helps in the preparation, but it's not until the actual race is experienced do you know how you will run that particular course.

Our lives certainly have rough terrains too, though often we don't know the ending point, as in the case of an actual running race. And just because you are a Christian doesn't give you immunity from hard times either. Jesus said to His disciples before His arrest, illegal trials, beatings, and crucifixion, "Here on earth you will have many trials and sorrows. But take heart, because I have overcome the world" (John 16:33 NLT). James, the half brother of Jesus, said in his letter to Jewish believers, "When troubles of any kind come your way, consider it an opportunity for great joy. For you know that when your faith is tested, your endurance has a chance to grow" (James 1:3 NLT). There's encouragement in the midst of tough times. The apostle Peter states in his first letter, "So if you are suffering in a manner that pleases God, keep on doing what is right, and trust your lives to the God who created you, for he will never fail you" (1 Peter 4:19 NLT).

Are you going through a difficult time in your life? Ask the Lord to give you grace and wisdom to persevere.

43

Is It Wrong to Lie?

Runners and fishermen have a common characteristic: they love to tell tales. Sadly, that commonality lends to the temptation of exaggeration. Fishermen stretch the truth by rounding up the length of their catch, and runners who want to appear faster tend to round down their time. Usually, their intentions are innocent, though the underlying motive is to look good to others.

Although many do not give thought to this, exaggeration is a form of lying, along with multiple other forms. Why do people lie? It is inherent in all of us and may very well be the most common sin. Ask any parent of a toddler. No one has to be taught how to lie. The reasons vary: greed, revenge, embarrassment, unable to deal with conflict. But the primary reason for lying is fear. There are plenty of stories in the Bible about people who told a lie or two. On two different occasions, Abraham used the same lie by misleading Pharaoh and King Abimelech into thinking Sarah was his sister when she was in fact his wife. He used a family connection as a half-truth to justify his story (Genesis 12:10–20 and 20:1–18). Joseph's brothers duped their father into thinking Joseph was killed by wild animals. When in fact, they bloodied his coat and threw him into a pit (Genesis 37). And false witnesses were brought in to testify against Jesus in a trial that wasn't even legal (Matthew 26:57–67).

Nothing good comes from lying. Some of the consequences are mistrust, telling more lies, damaging credibility and integrity. The Bible is very explicit as to how God views lying. In fact, it is one of the things God hates (Proverbs 6:16–19). Ephesians 4:25 (NASB) states, "Therefore, laying aside falsehood, speak truth, each one of you, with his neighbor, for we are members of one another." We are to speak the truth with love. God calls all Christians to live truthfully in every aspect of their lives. Is it always easy to tell the truth? No, but God will give the courage to do so.

When was the last time you lied? Do you know why? Have you made it right?

44

Anger

Uh-oh! The sun woke me up, but that was not a good sign. It meant I was probably late for a 5K I planned to run. My first thought was, *Why did no one call me?* (These were in the days before mobile phones. Landlines and pay phones were the only options.) I had planned to carpool with friends and eat breakfast afterward. It didn't take long for anger to well up in me. And the longer I dwelled on it, the angrier I became. It was rare for me to be a no-show. Looking at the clock, if I hurried. I could make the forty-five-minute drive to the race with maybe a few minutes to spare. I had already registered for the race. While driving, and speeding at that, I kept asking, Why didn't anyone take the time to call? Did they not care? Did they not wonder why I wasn't on time when I usually am? A close parking spot was found, and I was able to get to the start before the gun went off. Anger fueled me, not my usual prerace meal, and I ran one of my better race times! Later, I saw my friends at the finish. When I asked in a not-so-pleasant tone, "Why didn't anyone call me?" The answer I received was not the one expected. "You weren't where we were meeting, so we went on." More anger. At the least, I expected a "sorry" or some sort of apology. I was wrong by not sharing how I felt and realized I had a wrong expectation as well as having a lack of communication on my part. I did not plan ahead of time for a just-in-case wake-up call. Fortunately, I harbored no ill-will or bitterness.

Fast-forward years later when a triathlon I was participating in was canceled right before the start due to lightning. Needless to say, there were many angry athletes, even though refunds were offered. I was more disappointed than angry but worked through it by the time I arrived back home.

Anger is a powerful emotion and can become a deadly sin if not dealt with quickly. Even the Bible addresses this by saying, "And don't sin by letting anger control you. Don't let the sun go down while you are still angry, for anger gives a foothold to the devil" (Ephesians 4:26–27 NLT). Bitterness, jealousy, and gossip are just a few negative emotions that result in unresolved anger. And it is sobering to read that many incidences of anger result in murder. Seldom is there a headline about a murder where anger is not involved. Its's a stark reality of not only in today's world but also in biblical times, which is filled with real people in real-life situations and with real emotions, including anger. In fact, the first incident of anger in the Bible led to murder: Cain killing his brother, Abel. God's question to Cain was the first step in dealing with anger: acknowledgment. Cain never admitted his anger, and his jealousy got the best of him with lifelong consequences.

Read the following verses on anger: Proverbs 12:16, 15:1, 19:11 and James 1:19–20. Ask God to help and direct you with the situations that come up in life leading to anger, as well as with any unresolved anger issues, no matter how minor they seem.

45

Nature in All Its Glory

Trail running is starkly different from road running and certainly from running on a treadmill. There are many advantages to trail running: safety from vehicles, challenging courses, and a quieter atmosphere to name a few. It even develops greater strength in knees, ankles, and feet. But by far, the greatest advantage of running trails is observing nature. The Midwest offers an amazing variety, which includes four seasonal changes, like different channels on TV. Each season offers its own uniqueness. What beauty to behold when tall grasses encased in ice, looking like lab tubes, lined up for inspection and watching ice pellets bounce on a frozen trail, like marbles. The wonderful silence of new fallen snow early in the morning is difficult to describe. Spring offers the excitement of watching seemly deadness everywhere, and then to be in awe how quickly, with warming days, *boom*, new foliage appears as though it had always been there. In the summer, trails offer coolness of tree covering from the blazing sun. But watch out for fields of screams: poison ivy. (Why aren't animals allergic?) Autumn is as colorful in a different way from spring, as well as even having its own fragrance. Sadly, it often brings on the melancholy feelings of an approaching winter.

God created the world for us to enjoy and be good stewards of the earth we live on. And for those who don't believe in God as a Creator, and that everything, including us, is here by chance, the last five chapters in the book of Job include challenges by God to Job regarding creation. Here are also a few of my own questions I've pondered on and asked with amazement: Why do turkey buzzards spend so much time soaring in the sky? How fun it must be. How is it that geese know to fly in formation, and how is the leader selected and rotated? Bet they don't fight and argue about it! How is wildlife camouflaged in their environment along with the seasons? And how do those noisy cicadas know whether they are the thirteen- or seventeen-year type? The questions are endless.

Read Genesis 1.

46

Injuries

The Detroit Free Press Marathon was about three weeks away, and the tapering in my training had begun. It was then that my left knee began hurting. Having not run many marathons and never having a major running injury before, I stubbornly chose to continue my training regime rather than address the injury, especially if it meant taking some time off. Well, the knee pain didn't get better but worsened. Even a week before I was to leave, the pain was so bad. I knew if I rested for the week, I still wouldn't be able to complete the race. Sadly, I made the difficult choice not to run but went ahead and traveled to Detroit since I was staying with my aunt and uncle. As it turned out, I'm glad I went. Even though I was disappointed and upset about not running, I had a wonderful visit and learned a lot of family history.

Injuries may seem like an interference and a spoiler, but they can be beneficial, just like the trials in our lives. One is the squelching of pride. It was humbling to respond when others asked, "How did you do?" with a reply of "I didn't run," and then having to explain why not. We often think, during times of running, well, we're invincible, when *wham*, a pulled hamstring, tripping over a crack in the road, getting sick, or any number of circumstances happen. Second, injuries remind us of our limitations. And this is certainly true of those who began running earlier in life. Age has a way of catching up with us. And third, injuries cause a level of compassion for others you meet later who are injured, giving encouragement and even sometimes welcomed advice that helps a fellow runner get through their injury. One positive resulted from this injury. The visit with my aunt and uncle removed the disappointment and anger I had at myself for becoming injured at the wrong time.

Though the reasons for most of our trials are never seen, we can put our hope and trust in the Lord God, as Romans 8:28 (NLT) states, "And we know that God causes everything to work together for the good of those who love God and are called according to his purpose for them."

Has there been a setback in your life lately? Are you learning patience and seeking God's wisdom?

47

Grieving a Loss

As events unfolded during the 2013 Boston Marathon bombing and well afterward, I found myself somewhat obsessed with watching videos, interviews, eyewitness, and survivor stories. On several occasions, I experienced times of intense crying, more so than the normal sadness felt during tragic events. I wondered why. I was not directly involved, nor did I even know anyone running in the race that year. One day, I realized, much of the pain and sorrow I felt was because of my desire to be among fellow runners and the camaraderie that the running community brings. I was also grieving my own loss of not being able to run as I used to. I would sometimes cry while walking, as I would see a group running or cross paths with someone running solo. I also knew the end was drawing near when I would no longer be able to run anymore. I was having difficulty accepting the inevitable.

Losses will be inevitable in our lives, and how we respond will make a tremendous difference in our future. Grieving has specific stages that need to be worked through and addressed: a state of shock or disbelief, emotional release, loneliness and isolation, guilt, anger, disillusionment, then acceptance and reestablishment. Choosing not to face the pain can lead to bitterness, depression, or other such negative emotions. The Bible does not shy away from grief, sorrow, and despair. Jesus was called a man of sorrows, who is acquainted with grief (Isaiah 53:3). Two very comforting verses among many that show God does care are Psalm 34:18 (NLT), "The Lord is close to the broken hearted, he rescues those whose spirits are crushed" and Psalm 56:8 (NLT), "You keep track of all my sorrows. You've collected all my tears in your bottle. You have recorded each one in your book."

Have you worked through the steps of grieving in a recent loss?

48

Maintaining Focus

One particularly difficult race for a flatlander like me from Missouri is the Pikes Peak Ascent in Colorado Springs, Colorado. The race was not only physically challenging but mentally as well, especially the last three miles where the tree line ends, and the course becomes rocky and winding. There are also significant changes in altitude and weather. Since this was my first experience with any mountainous terrain, I quickly found out how deceiving and maddening switchbacks are. Switchback is a term used to describe the sharp zigzag pattern of a trail to ease hiking up a mountainside. On many occasions, I wrongly thought I was about to cross the finish line since I could see it and hear the announcer calling out finishers' names. I got excited and stepped up the pace (to a faster walk!). I encountered so many switchbacks. I was becoming discouraged, and my struggle to finish waivered too. I quickly learned that I needed to readjust my focus from anticipating the finish too soon and concentrate on the rocky terrain at hand.

Life is like that sometimes. We can become too focused on the end result rather than our present circumstances and not realize the Lord may have some refining or lessons for us to learn in the meantime.

Nehemiah was a man who maintained a balance between his goal and the obstacles he faced. A cupbearer by profession, he had a burden to repair the city walls and gates of Jerusalem. He received a leave of absence, diplomatic papers of permission, and supplies from King Artaxerxes. Word quickly spread in the region, including enemies. Just a few of Nehemiah's hindrances included lies from the opposition, organizing and assigning buildings sections to be repaired, and sometimes using less-skilled laborers along with the skilled craftsmen. There were also threats of attacks and lack of food. He always kept his "finish line" in sight and did what was necessary for the moment while maintaining his integrity. And in fifty-two days, the walls and gates were completed. The dedicated celebration of sacrifices and singing were such that "the joy of the people of Jerusalem could be heard far away" (Nehemiah 12:43).

What are some specific ways you can maintain focus in your life?

49

Mile 21

Mile 21 (Km 35) may be the most difficult part of a marathon. All runners will experience some level of pain at this point. This is when a runner relies on months of physical training and mental discipline. Why is Mile 21 so difficult? Because a runner has come too far to quit and give up (barring an unforeseen injury) and the finish line is not yet in sight. The last five miles seem like an eternity. It is much easier to quit than to persevere.

Twice In the fourth chapter of 2 Corinthians, the apostle Paul encourages the Corinthian Christians by using a phrase all runners have heard at one time or another: "Never give up." Paul makes it inclusive by saying, "We never give up" (verses 1 and 16). Throughout this chapter, the apostle talks about what seems to be life in the twenty-first century, not in early Roman times. "We are pressed on every side by troubles, but we are not crushed. We are perplexed, but not driven to despair. We are hunted down, but never abandoned by God. We get knocked down, but we are not destroyed" (verses 8 and 9 NLT). Later he adds, "For our present troubles are small and won't last very long. Yet they produce for us a glory that vastly outweighs them and will last forever" (verse 17 NLT).

Are you at a "Mile 21" in your life? Ask the Lord to give you the strength to persevere.

<h1 style="text-align:center">50</h1>

In Sight of the Finish Line

As the sight of the finish line becomes visible and the cheers of spectators increase, every runner does their best to pick up the pace and even attempt to sprint to the finish line. It's a wonderful site to behold and to experience. No words can adequately describe the joy and sense of accomplishment felt after crossing the finish line. Months of training and sacrifices have come to an end. As runners walk through chutes, they are handed their reward: a finisher's medal.

Before his impending execution, the apostle Paul expressed similar feelings about how he lived his life: "I have fought the good fight, I have finished the course, I have kept the faith: in the future there is laid up for me the crown of righteousness, which the Lord, the righteous Judge, will award me on that day; and not only to me but also to all who have loved His appearing" (2 Timothy 4:7–8 NASB). This encouragement of perseverance is just as applicable to Christians today as it was in the early first century.

Read how Jesus crossed His finish line of life in John 19:28–30 and Hebrews 12:2–3.

51

After the Finish

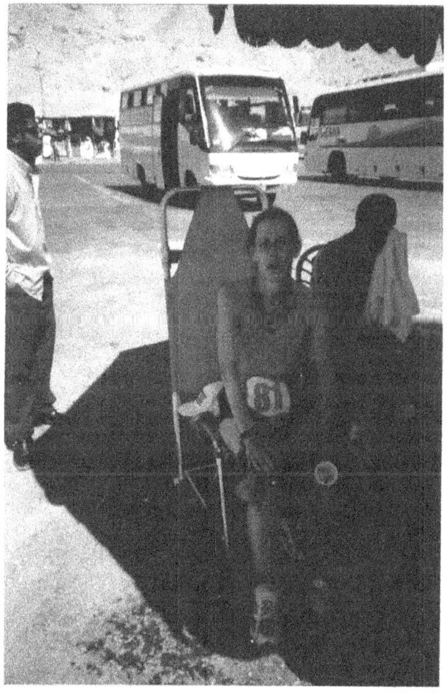

The Egyptian Marathon had proved to be one of the more difficult races I ran and not because of the terrain, which was a four-loop flat course. It was the temperature difference. February weather in the US Midwest is certainly not the same as in Luxor, Egypt. And I was not acclimated. The course had no shade, and running on an asphalt road probably added to the temperature. Even though the race began early morning, I'm a slower runner. And since the marathon had few runners, the course director was in the process of closing down the race and allowing traffic back on the road as I neared the finish line. My friend, who ran the half marathon, had to look for water as I was beet red and dehydrated. I was able to find a shady place that had a chair and slumped my poor body into it. Admittedly, I was rather disappointed that there were no food items, and the only activity was that of volunteers putting things away. I was tired, hot, and hungry. There was to be a postmarathon celebration that evening, and I really didn't have any high expectations. When we arrived though, I was astounded at the massive banquet set up with food galore. There were tables set up with the names of countries represented that day. Not only that, men and women performed traditional dances, and sport directors from several Middle Eastern countries spoke and presented the awards. This was a much bigger deal than I had ever anticipated, grandiose hospitality. A smiling face replaced my disappointment and tired countenance and body. I was also able to visit with other runners and hear of their experiences.

With time, pain endured disappears. The apostle Paul said in one of his letters that accurately describes a similar experience for Christians. Romans 8:18 (NASB) says, "For I consider that the sufferings of this present time are not worthy to be compared with the glory that is to be revealed to us." All Christians will have eternity to share their marathon of life with fellow believers. We can be sure that eternity will be filled with even more joy and excitement of meeting Jesus and feasting at His finisher's banquet.

Read Revelation 21 and 22.

52

The Winner's Crown

Competition has one main purpose: running to win the prize. Regardless of what it is, this is the focus of the runner. The lesser-known Isthmian Games held in Corinth, Greece, may have been the venue where the apostle Paul watched or at least was in the area when they were held. Unlike races nowadays, only the winner received the prize, a perishable crown made of celery leaves! There were no second or third places or age categories, so everyone ran all out to win. It is here where Paul shares his spiritual word pictures using running to encourage fellow followers of Jesus Christ. In his first letter to the Corinthian Church, he said, "Do you not know that in a race all the runners run, but only one gets the prize? Run in such a way as to get the prize. Everyone who competes in the games goes into strict training. They do it to get a crown that will not last, but we do it to get a crown that will last forever" (chapter 9, verses 24 through 25 NIV).

All followers of Jesus Christ will receive various crowns (*stephanos*) at the end of their race of life. The crown of life is given when we patiently endured trials and temptations (James 1:12). The humble are crowned with victory (Psalm 149:4). And there is the crown of glory for those leaders in the churches who serve faithfully (1 Peter 5:4). One of the most significant crowns mentioned in the Bible is one we *don't* have to put on, the crown of thorns Jesus Christ wore the day of His crucifixion. Roman soldiers mocked and beat Him as

He wore that crown, as well as a purple robe, before being led to the cross where he would die for sinners (1 Timothy 1:15). This particular crown did not have a beautiful appearance, but it represents Jesus's victory over death. "But thank God! He gives us the victory over sin and death through our Lord Jesus Christ" (1 Corinthians 15:57 NLT).

Will you be receiving a crown upon your death?

53

Rewards

Unlike the ancient games, where only the winner was crowned, most marathons now give at least a finisher's medal to those completing the 26.2-mile course. Also, a T-shirt and a bag of complimentary items donated by various companies are common with many races, regardless of the distance. Marathons and races of lesser distance have some sort of prize, not only for the overall victor but some sort of reward for other categories, such as winners in age groups. Olympians train to win the gold medal. Silver and bronze medals are also awarded. Many elite runners often enter races that offer monetary prizes. Winning could also result in a state championship for a high schooler in track or cross-country. Those who win overall or run faster often receive a better reward compared to ones who only finish.

Followers of Jesus Christ will also receive various rewards at the end of their race of life. In the areas of giving, fasting, and praying, our Father, who sees those things, will reward us when done in secret or privately (Matthew 6:4, 6, 17, 18). Ephesians 6:8 states, "Remember the Lord will reward each of us for the good we do…" And Jesus, in His well-known Sermon on the Mount, encourages and promises His followers, saying, "God blesses you when people mock you and persecute you, and lie about you, and say all sorts of evil things against you because you are my followers. Be happy about it! Be very glad! For a great reward awaits you in heaven" (Matthew 5:12 NLT).

What is your motivation for the good deeds you are doing? Are they done to honor God and to store up treasures in heaven (Matthew 6:19–21), or are you wanting to look good and be impressed by people?

54

Book of Results

Egyptian Marathon Results - Sex Categorized

Event No.   **12**   *Da*
Race Kind :   **Marathon**
Type/Name :   **Marathon**

Female Results - Marathon

Place	No	Time	Name	D.O.B	Country	Club
1	82	03:24:48	Suzette Vermaak	1968	SA	
2	83	03:57:45	Skrivanek Carissa	1984	USA	
3	78	04:01:50	Rebe Ute	1968	GER	
4	77	04:11:29	Dahl Martina	1956	GER	
5	85	04:18:50	Rebecca Byerly	0	USA	
6	256	04:20:28	Zohra Merabet	1950	ALG	
7	79	04:30:29	Ostboll Solveig	1956	NOR	
8	81	05:06:02	Susan Merrell	1956	USA	
9	76	05:25:23	Grofke Ulrike	1953	GER	
10	80	05:40:10	Ritz Mary	1954	USA	

01/03/2005

In the first decades of modern marathon running, each runner would either be mailed a result book or a post card, indicating their placement in the marathon they ran. Nowadays, runners can know their results much more quickly, within a few days or hours. Results are posted online with each runner's name, bib number, and their time recorded. This is the proof that a registered runner finished the marathon.

Revelation 20:11–15 speaks of a similar concept, the Book of Life. Verse 15 states one of the most sobering verses in the Bible, "And anyone whose name was not found recorded in the Book of Life was thrown in the Lake of Fire" (NLT). Though many people question how God can send anyone to hell, in actuality, God never sends anyone there purposely. He "wants everyone to be saved and to understand the truth" (1 Timothy 2:4) via the salvation Jesus Christ offers or sadly accept the consequences of eternal punishment for their sins. Just as a registered finisher can point to their name in the book of results, every follower of Jesus Christ can have full assurance that their name is written in God's Book of Life.

Those in hell will be forever separated from God's presence (1 Thessalonians 1:9). James 1:17 (NLT) gives a clue to what hell will be like: "Whatever is good and perfect is a gift coming down to us from God our Father, who created the lights in heaven. He never changes or cast a shifting shadow." So that would logically mean, anything that comes from God will not be in hell. Consider that hell will be dark because God is light (1 John 1:15). There will be no friends, family, or companionship (Genesis 2:18), and there will be no nature of any sort (Romans 8:20–21). And worse of all, there will be no more opportunities to change one's mind regarding God's salvation (Hebrews 9:27–28). That's forever regretting.

In stark contrast, heaven will be a place of no evil

(Revelation 21:27), no sorrow, pain, or death (Revelation 21:4). Heaven and earth will be brand-new (Revelation 21:1), as well as our bodies (2 Corinthians 5:1) and fellowship with Jesus *forever!*

Read the parable of Lazarus and the rich man (Luke 16:19–31).

About the Author

Susan Merrell is a first-time author. Her passion for international travel, research, and the wonders of nature, combined with her running experiences, give this book a unique perspective of the Christian life. She became a member of the Seven Continents Club in 2005.

www.ingramcontent.com/pod-product-compliance
Lightning Source LLC
Chambersburg PA
CBHW050751160726
48004CB00002B/508

INTRODUCTION

If you've ever found yourself asking *"Why me"* when facing adversity, know that you are not alone. According to the <u>Centers for Disease Control and Prevention</u> (CDC), *"Half of all U.S. children have experienced some kind of trauma in the form of abuse, neglect, violence or challenging household circumstances—and 35 percent of children have experienced more than one type of traumatic event."* Challenges are a natural part of life, however, the key to success is how you respond to them. In this book, we will explore overcoming obstacles and cultivating resilience, especially for young girls and women facing tough times.

In a world of challenges and uncertainties, I believe resilience begins with three core pillars: LOVE - LIFT - LEAD. These guiding principles serve as the foundation of this book, aimed at inspiring and empowering young girls and women as they navigate life's trials and tribulations.

Resilience, the ability to turn pain into power, is a transformative force that shapes our responses to adversity. Through my experiences, I have learned the art of resilience, overcoming significant obstacles with unwavering determination.

I am Shantay Carter, also known as *The Nurse Philanthropist,* I have established and am currently heading three non-profit organizations. As a survivor of COVID-19, I have faced the fear of the unknown firsthand. The losses of my beloved grandmother and father led me into deep despair, yet I found the courage to persevere. Even in the face of losing my job, I refused to be defined by setbacks, choosing instead to channel my pain into strength.

To conquer adversity, one must approach challenges with intentionality. While feeling overwhelmed during tough times is natural, remember that the strength to overcome lies within you. Resilience is the key to surviving and thriving in the face of adversity. By embracing the power of love, uplifting others, and leading by example, you can harness your struggles and transform them into sources of strength.

This book is a testament to the resilience and power of all young women and girls facing their battles. You can overcome any obstacle that comes your way. Through practical guidance centered around love, lifting others, and leadership, this book will support you in navigating through tough times and emerging stronger on the other side. The world eagerly awaits your brilliance. Don't wait! Start reading this book today, rise above adversity, and shine brightly.

RESILIENCE

> *"Character cannot be developed in ease and quiet. Only through experience of trial and suffering can the soul be strengthened, ambition inspired, and success achieved."* -
> **Helen Keller**

I am a New York native and a Binghamton University alumnus. I wear many hats - as a bestselling author, three-time non-profit founder, professional speaker, and a registered nurse. People often seek my advice on launching successful non-profit organizations, but what they may not know is that my first non-profit venture, over 14 years ago, stemmed from my struggles.

I am driven by a deep-seated passion for giving back through mentorship, particularly in empowering young girls and women to overcome adversity with the necessary tools.

In my journey, I have learned the vital role of confidence and resilience in facing challenges head-on. I am dedicated to presenting the best version of myself and acknowledge the significance of fostering connections and collaboration and instilling confidence in others. My ultimate mission is to ensure that all girls and women have equal access to opportunities that have shaped my path to success.

Before I go into my three principles to overcome adversity, I want to first discuss the importance of turning pain into power as a prerequisite to my three principles.

Pain

Pain, they say, is a signal that something is amiss within your body, a warning that all is not well. For me, this pain stemmed from the traumas and losses I endured over the past three years. Sometimes, the suffering we endure ultimately strengthens us and helps us grow. We learn to harness our pain and turn it into our power, becoming resilient.

Throughout these three years, I faced various challenges and pain, especially during the pandemic. I suffered the loss of loved ones, friends, colleagues, and even my job.

Allow me to tell you a little more about me. As mentioned, I am a survivor of Covid-19. During the Pandemic, New York and the rest of the world went into lockdown. I contracted the virus from a patient at work, and I was the first person out of my family and friends to contract it. Before my diagnosis, I believe we thought Covid was a common cold and wouldn't be that bad.

On March 17th, 2020, feeling extremely unwell, I sought urgent care, and as a result tested positive on March 20th, 2020. I battled the illness for two long months, gripped by fear of the unknown and uncertainty over my survival. I was blessed to have recovered when many others did not. I realized that my mission was not yet complete. I committed to prioritizing my health, adopting better eating habits, and increasing physical activity.

Following this, I tragically lost my grandmother on June 7th, 2020. She was my inspiration and role model for becoming a nurse, having worked multiple jobs, and migrating from Jamaica to ensure a better life for her children. Though devastated by her passing, I found solace in knowing she was no longer suffering.

The pain intensified when I unexpectedly lost my father on May 21st, 2021. I got the call while I was at work. Traumatized and anxious, I felt like my world had collapsed. The loss of a parent is indescribable, and I found myself spiraling into depression and seeking therapy to cope with my grief. My therapist guided me through the initial stages of grief, helping me address the pain and trauma I endured.

Further turmoil struck when I lost my job in October 2021, after 21 years as a bedside nurse. Now this pain came from the place that I least expected it. The profession that I love, had lost its integrity and had become unethical. I was angry. I wondered who I was without nursing. It was all I knew. I was left asking myself what happened to the *care* in healthcare? How do I overcome adversity and turn my pain into my power? What was going to be my next move?

Transfer Pain to Power

I am aware that many of you may resonate with the trauma and loss I have faced in the past three years.

As someone perceived as strong, the expectation to move on without acknowledging the pain was overwhelming. Thus, I ask, how does one cultivate resilience in the face of adversity? Overcoming adversity has always been about incorporating three principles in your life to show up as your best self. I call it my 3 L's- Love, Lift, and Lead. Love: Self-love to rediscover my identity and purpose, Leadership: developing strategies to overcome challenges, and Lift: channeling my pain into a strength by uplifting others.

Life is full of challenges and obstacles that can bring us pain and suffering. It is easy to let these unwanted changes and losses define us and drag us down. However, it is important to remember that we have the power to turn our pain into something positive and overcome all obstacles.

Turning pain into power is about finding the strength and courage to overcome adversity and use our experiences to make a positive impact on ourselves and others. By practicing love, leading, and lifting others, we can create a ripple effect of positivity and prevent others from suffering in the same way we have. Through these actions, we can turn our pain into power and emerge stronger and more resilient than ever before. In the end, it is not about the challenges we face but how we choose to respond to them that truly defines us. Let us all strive to turn our pain into power, cultivate resilience, and create a brighter future for ourselves and those around us.

In the next chapter, we will discuss embracing love to overcome adversity. Love is a powerful force that can help us navigate through life's toughest challenges. When we open our hearts to love, we can find strength, support, and solace during adversity. Love can heal wounds, mend broken hearts, and bring light to even the darkest of days.

NOTES

Transforming Pain
into Strength

> *"The most authentic thing about us is our capacity to create, to overcome, to endure, to transform, to love, and to be greater than our suffering."* **-Ben Okri**

The concept of turning pain into power is all about discovering the inner strength and courage to conquer challenges and using our experiences to have a positive impact on ourselves and those around us. By love, I am referring to practicing self-love, displaying love to others, and creating positive influences to prevent others from experiencing the same pain. Through these actions, we can transform our pain into power and emerge stronger and more resilient.

Self-Love

Everything begins with self-love. Loving oneself is crucial because you are valuable and enough, but you must realize it first. Self-love is the foundation to overcome any challenges. It means loving yourself, including your flaws. It's about believing in and treating yourself with kindness. Self-love is thinking positively about yourself and focusing on your strengths instead of limitations. It's about understanding and knowing who you are. Knowing you have a purpose and consistently improving yourself, even when faced with difficulties.

Self-care and self-compassion are essential for overall well-being. In a world where self-criticism and negativity are common, it is vital to prioritize taking care of yourself. By practicing self-love and self-compassion, you can develop a positive relationship with yourself, leading to better mental health and emotional resilience.

After losing my job, I knew that I needed to rebuild and regroup. I called this time my *"rebirth."* I knew that I would rise through the ashes like a phoenix someday. During that time, I looked for ways to level up, personally and professionally. I wanted to make myself more marketable and desirable in the nursing profession.

During the seven months that I was unemployed, I achieved the following:

- Obtained my nursing license in five different states
- Keynote speaker for ANA-NY in 2021
- Nurse Entrepreneur of the Year from GNYC BNA in 2021
- Became a member of Chi Eta Phi Sorority, Incorporated in 2022, which reignited my love for the profession, erased my anger towards it, and gave me a second chance to do what I love
- Keynote Speaker for the 2022 North East Regional Conference of Chi Eta Phi Sorority, Incorporated
- Became a member of Sigma Theta Tau International Nursing Honor Society in 2022

All these accomplishments led me to my new job in an outpatient neurology office, which I now love.

Losing my job was heartbreaking, but I couldn't drown in my tears. I had to turn that pain into something positive. To achieve this, I had to love myself and believe in myself. I had to be willing to lead and set an example for others. I had to stand up for what I believed in and stay true to who I was. As the saying goes, *"You have to stand for something, or you will fall for anything."* Leveling up and staying true to my core values led me to my present job, where I am very satisfied.

Loving Others

In addition to self-love, love, and relationships are the cornerstone of our emotional well-being. From the support of our family, friends, and community to the importance of nurturing healthy connections, love plays a vital role in our happiness and fulfillment. It is crucial to show love and guidance to the younger generation, as they are the future leaders of our world.

In 2010, I went through a difficult breakup that left me feeling shattered and lost. The toxic relationship drained me emotionally and spiritually and caused me to question my self-worth. The aftermath of the breakup led me to a dark place of anger, hurt, and betrayal, which affected all my relationships. It was a challenging time when I felt isolated and overwhelmed.

Reflecting on that period now, I realize that I was experiencing depression without recognizing it. Mental abuse can be just as damaging as other forms of abuse, and breaking free from it is a difficult task. I knew I had to make a change, to stop playing the victim and take charge of my life. With the intervention and support of true friends and family, I was able to navigate through the darkness and transform my pain into strength. My friends went to my parents on my behalf, which gave me a great circle of love for me to bounce back.

Through this experience, I learned to foster healthy relationships and channel negative energy into something positive. Love and support from those around us are essential in overcoming adversity and finding fulfillment in life.

It was through the love and guidance of my loved ones that I was able to heal and rebuild myself. They showed me that I was deserving of love and respect, and they helped me rediscover my self-worth. With their support, I was able to let go of the pain and hurt from the past relationship and focus on cultivating healthy and loving connections. All you need is one person to believe in you when you are going through your adversity. Having that person believe in you, will give you the strength and courage to believe in yourself. I am blessed that my friends believed in me.

I realized that love is not just about romantic relationships but also about the love we share with our friends, family, and community. It is about showing compassion, empathy, and kindness to others, and in return, receiving the same love and support. Love is a powerful force that can heal wounds, mend broken hearts, and bring joy and happiness into our lives.

Through the power of love, I was able to transform my pain into strength and emerge as a stronger and more resilient person. I now understand the importance of self-love, compassion, and nurturing relationships in fostering a positive and fulfilling life. Love truly has the power to heal, inspire, and empower us to overcome any challenges that come our way.

Embrace Love to Overcome Adversity

As I continue my journey of self-love and love for others, I realize the impact that love has on our lives. Love is not just a feeling but a force that drives us to be better, overcome obstacles, and spread positivity in the world. Through self-love and love for others, we can create a ripple effect of kindness and compassion that can change lives and bring about positive change in our communities.

I am grateful for the lessons I have learned through my experiences of pain and transformation. They have taught me the value of love and the resilience that comes from embracing it. I am committed to continuing to practice self-love, to nurture my relationships, and to spread love wherever I go. Love is the most powerful force in the world, and by embracing it, we can unlock our full potential and create a brighter, more loving world for ourselves and those around us.

Self-Reflection

As you navigate the ups and downs of life and relationships, it's essential to take a moment to reflect on how love influences your world. These self-reflection questions are here to help you explore your relationship with yourself and others and to understand the power of love in your life. By diving into these questions, you might uncover new insights and perspectives that can guide you on your path to self-discovery and growth. Grab a pen and paper, or open a *Notes* app, and dive into these questions. It's time to explore the impact of love in your life and relationships.

1. How do you prioritize self-love and self-care in your daily routine?
2. What are some ways in which you show love and appreciation for yourself regularly?
3. Are you able to set healthy boundaries in your relationships to protect your emotional well-being?
4. How do you communicate your needs and expectations in your relationships to ensure mutual respect and understanding?
5. Do you believe that you deserve love and respect from others, or do you struggle with feelings of unworthiness?

6. How do you handle conflicts and disagreements in your relationships in a way that promotes understanding and growth?

7. Have you forgiven yourself for past mistakes and shortcomings, and do you allow yourself to move forward with self-compassion?

8. Are you able to recognize and address toxic patterns or behaviors in your relationships that may hinder your emotional growth?

9. How do you show appreciation and gratitude for the love and support you receive from others in your life?

10. Have you taken the time to reflect on your values and beliefs about love and how they influence your relationships with others?

NOTES

EMPOWERMENT IN ACTION

"Start where you are. Use what you have.
Do what you can." **-Toby Hazlewood**

In a society where competition is fierce and opportunities are limited, individuals need to support and uplift one another. This notion of lifting others, rather than holding them back, is crucial for personal growth and collective success. This chapter will explore the concept of "LIFT" - the act of reaching back to pull up the next person coming behind us.

Benefits of Lifting Others Up

The crab-in-the-barrel mentality, where individuals in a group try to bring down those who are trying to succeed, is a hindrance to progress and prosperity. By embracing a mindset of lifting others, we create a culture of collaboration, support, and empowerment. Sometimes, we may be the crab that is holding others and ourselves back, perhaps making poor choices in life, socially, or academically. When we see others working together and collaborating to help others get ahead, we must follow suit. Instead of pulling one another down, we should be helping each other by supporting and encouraging those who strive for more.

Picture yourself as a teenage girl in a crowded high school hallway, surrounded by your classmates. Among them, there is a girl named Mia who is determined to excel in her studies and make a positive impact on the world.

As Mia strives to achieve her goals, she notices a troubling trend among her peers. Whenever someone starts to stand out or shine, others begin to gossip, criticize, or bring them down to maintain their status quo.

Mia realizes that this toxic behavior only holds everyone back and prevents them from reaching their full potential. Instead of getting caught up in the negativity, she decides to take a different approach.

Every day, Mia tries to lift her classmates and offer words of encouragement, support, and kindness. She shows them that there is a world of possibilities beyond the limited mindset of jealousy and competition.

One day, a crisis hits the school when a beloved teacher falls ill, and the students must come together to support each other. Mia steps up, organizing a fundraiser and rallying her classmates to show their solidarity.

As they work together towards a common goal, the students realize the power of unity and collaboration. They see that by lifting each other, they can achieve more than they ever thought possible.

From that day on, the students understood mutual respect and support. Together, they learned that through mutual respect and support, they could achieve so much more than they ever could alone. They knew that by fostering a culture of support and collaboration, they could all reach greater heights and make a difference in the lives of those around them. And so, with hearts full of determination and minds set on making a positive impact, the students set out to conquer new challenges, knowing that together, they were unstoppable.

Although this story is fiction, Mia's example teaches us that by helping each other succeed, we can all reach greater heights and create a positive impact on the world around us.

One key element of the concept of "LIFT" is that by helping others succeed, we benefit. When we support and uplift those around us, we create a network of allies who can offer guidance, mentorship, and growth opportunities. This sense of community and camaraderie fosters a positive environment where everyone has the chance to thrive.

Furthermore, lifting others can cause a chain reaction, inspiring others to do the same. When individuals see the impact of their actions in helping someone else succeed, they are motivated to continue the cycle of support and empowerment. This creates a culture of generosity and kindness that can transform entire communities.

An example of the power of "LIFT" can be seen in entrepreneurship. Successful business leaders often attribute their success to the mentors and supporters who helped them along the way. By paying it forward and offering guidance to aspiring entrepreneurs, they can give back and uplift the next generation of innovators.

Are you ready to LIFT?

In conclusion, the concept of "LIFT" is essential for personal growth, professional success, and societal progress. By reaching back to pull up the next person coming behind us, we create a culture of collaboration, support, and empowerment. Let us strive to break free from the crab-in-the-barrel mentality and embrace a mindset of lifting others, for in doing so; we elevate not only ourselves but all those around us.

Now, let's shift our focus from the inspiring concept of lifting others to some thoughtful self-reflection questions. These questions are like a mirror, helping you see how you support and uplift those around you. Take a moment to ponder these questions and think about how you can bring more "LIFT" into your daily life. It's a chance to discover more about yourself and how you can make a positive impact on your friends, family, and community. Dive into these questions and explore the power of empowerment in action.

"We've got a responsibility to live up to the legacy of those who came before us, by doing all that we can to help those who come after us." - **Michelle Obama**

Self-Reflection

1. Have I actively sought opportunities to support and uplift others in my personal and professional life?
2. How have I contributed to creating a culture of collaboration and empowerment in my community or workplace?
3. In what ways have I recognized and celebrated the achievements and successes of those around me?
4. Have I ever found myself falling into a mindset of competition or jealousy instead of lifting others? If so, how can I work to change that mindset?
5. What impact have my actions had on those I have supported and uplifted? How have I seen them grow or succeed as a result?
6. How do I feel when I see others reaching out to help someone in need or offering support to those striving for success?
7. What steps can I take to further incorporate the concept of "LIFT" into my daily interactions and relationships?
8. Do I actively seek out mentorship opportunities to help guide and support others on their journeys?
9. How can I continue to inspire and motivate those around me to embrace the mindset of lifting others?

10. How has lifting others positively impacted my personal growth and development?

NOTES

MAKING A LASTING IMPACT

"It took me quite a long time to develop a voice, and now that I have it, I am not going to be silent."

- Madeleine Albright

In the face of adversity, we have the power to transform pain into purpose through the lens of leadership. As girls and women navigating life's challenges, we possess the resilience and strength to overcome obstacles and emerge stronger than before. We can create a path toward empowerment and fulfillment by harnessing our personal experiences and channeling negative energy into positive action. Through my journey of turning pain into power through leadership, I have learned valuable lessons in resilience, determination, and the transformative impact of embracing challenges. Join me as we explore how we can use our unique voices and leadership abilities to inspire and empower others and in doing so, make a lasting impact on the world around us.

Difficult circumstances may arise, but resilient individuals endure. As I've stated, after a painful breakup, it was the support and care of others that empowered me to act. As a means of channeling that negative energy into something positive, I started to think of everything I wanted to do in my life but had never got the chance. One thing I remembered that I always wanted to do was to start an organization that would help young girls and women. This was the beginning of my leadership. In this chapter, we will discuss how you can use leadership to turn pain into power.

Discovering Your Leadership Potential and Unique Voice ("A Voice to Lead")

As a young girl, I experienced pain and challenges that seemed insurmountable. But instead of letting those negative experiences define me, I made a conscious decision to turn that pain into my power through leadership. I realized that I could transform my struggles into something positive and impactful.

One night, in a moment of clarity, I decided to start an organization that would help young girls and women like me. I wanted to create a support system for those who felt lost and misguided, just as I once did. Thus, Women of Integrity, Inc. (WOI) was born. The name symbolized strength, integrity, and empowerment - qualities I wanted to instill in myself and others.

Through WOI, I channeled my pain into purpose. I found fulfillment in empowering and educating women of all ages and backgrounds. The organization not only helped me heal mentally but also allowed me to discover my own self-worth and inner strength. I learned that validation comes from within and that I had the power to shape my destiny.

Starting a non-profit organization is a challenging task, but I was determined to contribute to my community and support women. I had to put in a lot of effort, use my past experiences, and network extensively to make Women of Integrity a success. Despite facing numerous obstacles and setbacks, I never gave up and kept pushing forward. In my mind, failure was not an option. I relied on Google University, my experience as a Resident Assistant at Binghamton University, and my nursing background to guide me.

In the early stages of WOI, I had many late nights. There were a lot of negative responses, and our first prom dress drive was a failure. However, I refused to give up. I persisted, networked, and built up the organization. What began as a simple idea in my notebook has grown into a successful, award-winning organization. Over the years, we have been fortunate to help hundreds of women, particularly young women.

My journey from pain to power through leadership is a testament to the transformative impact of turning adversity into opportunity. As young girls, you may face your struggles and setbacks, but remember that you have the power within you to rise above them. Embrace your challenges as opportunities for growth and change. Believe in your ability to make a difference, both in your own life and in the lives of others. Remember, you are Destined for Greatness!

In the words of Winston Churchill, *"The positive thinker sees the invisible, feels the intangible, and achieves the impossible."* Let this be a guiding principle as you navigate life's ups and downs. Embrace your pain, transform it into power, and use your leadership skills to create a positive impact in the world. You have the potential to inspire others, just as I have been inspired by my journey. Let your story be a beacon of hope and empowerment for all those who follow in your footsteps.

Leadership

One of the key aspects of being a leader is the ability to inspire and motivate others. By sharing personal challenges and how they overcame them, leaders can show others that obstacles can be overcome with determination and resilience. For example, Nelson Mandela's long struggle against apartheid in South Africa inspired millions around the world to fight against injustice and oppression.

Furthermore, facing and overcoming challenges can also lead to the development of innovative ideas and solutions. Leaders who have experienced adversity firsthand are often more open to thinking outside the box and trying new approaches. For instance, Steve Jobs' experience of being fired from Apple in the 1980s led him to start a new company, NeXT, which led to his return to Apple and the development of groundbreaking products like the iPhone and iPad.

Sharing personal challenges can also help raise awareness about important issues and inspire others to act. Leaders need to be empathetic and vulnerable. Leaders who are open about their struggles can help reduce stigma and encourage others to seek help and support. For example, Oprah Winfrey's openness about her childhood trauma and struggles with weight and body image has inspired millions to speak out about their own experiences and seek help.

Steps to Overcome Difficulty Through Transferring Pain into Leadership:

By following the steps below and embracing the power of transferring pain into leadership, you can strive to make a positive impact in your communities and beyond. Reflecting on your experiences and challenges can not only help you grow as an individual but also inspire others to overcome their difficulties and reach their full potential.

Take a moment for self-reflection and consider how you can apply these principles in your life to create a brighter future for yourself and those around you.

5 Steps to Transform Pain and Lead

1. Acknowledge Your Pain: Recognize and accept the challenges you are facing but view them as opportunities for growth and transformation.
2. Reflect and Learn: Take time to reflect on your experiences and identify the lessons you can learn from them to develop your leadership skills.

3. Set Goals and Act: Define your purpose and set clear goals to channel your pain into positive action, whether through community projects, leadership programs, or volunteering.
4. Seek Support: Surround yourself with supportive and positive individuals who can offer guidance, mentorship, and encouragement as you navigate through difficulties.
5. Lead by Example: Use your journey of overcoming pain to inspire and empower others. Sharing your story of resilience and transformation to help fellow women and young girls facing similar struggles.

Are you ready to lead?

Being a leader is not only about achieving goals and targets but also about facing challenges and adversity with courage and resilience. Personal challenges can shape leadership qualities, champion innovative ideas, raise awareness, and inspire others to achieve their full potential. Leaders who are vulnerable and honest about their own experiences can truly make a difference in the lives of those around them.

I turned my pain into power through leadership by starting an organization called Women of Integrity, Inc. to help other young girls with similar challenges. Creating

Women of Integrity, Inc. saved my life. It helped me become a better woman, friend, daughter, sister, and nurse. Women Of Integrity, Inc. helped heal me mentally. It made me strengthen my self-worth and understand that I should never allow someone else to validate me; only I can validate myself. After seeing the positive impact of Women of Integrity, Inc., I also started Men of Integrity, Inc., and co-founded Nurses of Integrity. I transformed my pain and created a positive impact and so can you.

As we come to the end of our discussion on turning challenges into opportunities through leadership, it's time to pause and reflect. By pondering these questions, you can gain insight into how you can use your stories and abilities to make a difference in the lives of those around you. Take a moment to reflect on your experiences and consider how you can grow as a compassionate and inspiring leader.

Self-Reflection

1. How have you witnessed the power of leadership in your life or the lives of those around you?
2. Can you think of a time when you turned a difficult situation or personal challenge into a positive opportunity through leadership? What did you learn from that experience?

3. What do you believe are the most important qualities or skills for effective leadership when facing tough times and inspiring others?

4. Have you ever felt unsure about your ability to lead or make a difference when dealing with obstacles? How can you boost your confidence and resilience as a leader?

5. How can you use your own unique voice and life experiences to uplift and support peers, especially young girls and young adults who may be going through similar struggles?

6. How do you define success in leadership when it comes to transforming hardships into strength and creating a positive impact in your community?

7. Think about a leader who has inspired you by overcoming challenges with courage and resilience. What lessons can you apply from their story to your journey as a leader?

8. How can you continue to develop your leadership skills and grow as an empathetic and empowering leader for yourself and others?

9. What steps can you take to establish a network of support or a community that empowers and encourages young people facing difficulties, like the organization Women of Integrity, Inc.?

10. Reflect on the quote by Madeleine Albright: *"It took me quite a long time to develop a voice, and now that I have it, I am not going to be silent."* How does this quote resonate with your journey of finding your voice and using it to uplift and motivate others through leadership? How are you using your voice to lead?

NOTES

THE KEY TO UNLOCKING YOUR POTENTIAL AND ACHIEVING SUCCESS

> *"Believe you can and you're halfway there."*
> **- Theodore Roosevelt**

Have you ever wondered how someone can go from one career path to starting a successful non-profit organization? Let me tell you, it all starts with confidence and believing in yourself.

We've covered the effective ways to transform your pain into power by embracing love, lifting others, and leading the way. With these strategies in place, you can overcome any obstacle that comes your way and achieve success every time.

In addition, confidence is a key ingredient for success in life. Whether it is in personal relationships, academic pursuits, or professional endeavors, having confidence can make all the difference in overcoming adversity and achieving long-term success.

Confidence: A Necessity for Long-Term Success

Confidence is not only about feeling good about oneself; it is about having a belief in one's abilities and skills. It is about having the courage to take risks, push oneself out of one's comfort zone, and face challenges head-on. Without confidence, it is easy to become discouraged when faced with obstacles and setbacks. However, with confidence, one can approach challenges with a positive attitude and a determination to succeed.

Confidence over Setbacks

Confidence helps individuals bounce back from setbacks: In life, we will inevitably face setbacks and failures. However, individuals with confidence are better equipped to bounce back from these setbacks. They can see failure as a learning opportunity and to persevere in the face of adversity.

As I mentioned, I started Women of Integrity, Inc., out of necessity. After going through a tough breakup and falling into a dark place, I realized that I needed to make a change. With the support of my family and friends, I turned my pain into power and created something positive out of a negative situation. It is my confidence and self-belief that I continue to impact lives through all three of the non-profits I started.

Confidence Takes Risk

Confidence allows individuals to take risks: One of the main reasons why confidence is key to overcoming adversity and achieving success is that it allows individuals to take risks. When you have confidence in yourself and your abilities, you are more likely to take on new challenges and try new things. This willingness to take risks can lead to new opportunities and growth.

Confidence and Success

Confidence attracts success: Confidence is also attractive to others. When you exude confidence, you are more likely to be seen as a leader and to attract opportunities for success. People are drawn to those who are confident and self-assured, making it easier to form meaningful relationships and to advance in one's career and life.

Through my non-profit, I have been able to achieve success, such as becoming an award-winning nurse, best-selling author, empowerment leader, and TEDx speaker. All of this was possible because I believed in myself. I was intentional in my actions, surrounded myself with a strong support system, and took advantage of opportunities to better myself.

Remember, to be successful; you must have confidence in yourself, be willing to make changes, and be strategic in your decisions. Believe in yourself, know your worth, and never be afraid to chase your dreams. Confidence truly is the key to success.

Embrace Challenges Confidently

Believing in yourself and having confidence in your abilities can make all the difference in achieving your goals and making a positive impact in the world. With an optimistic mindset and determination, you can turn your pain into power, overcome any obstacle that comes your way, and create something truly remarkable. Have faith in yourself, take risks, and never give up on your dreams. Success is within your reach, and with confidence as your guide, you can achieve anything you set your mind to.

As we come to the end of our discussion on the power of confidence, remember that believing in yourself is the first step towards achieving your dreams and making a positive impact. With determination and a positive mindset, you can overcome any challenge and turn your struggles into strengths. Now, take a moment to reflect on your journey and consider how you can continue to build your confidence and reach new heights in your personal and professional life.

Self-Reflection

1. What are my strengths and accomplishments that I can remind myself of when facing challenges?
2. How do I react to setbacks or failures, and how can I reframe those experiences to build resilience and confidence?

3. In what areas do I tend to doubt myself the most, and what steps can I take to boost my confidence in those areas?

4. How do I talk to myself internally when faced with a difficult situation, and how can I change negative self-talk to more positive and empowering language?

5. What practices or activities help me feel more confident and capable, and how can I incorporate more of these into my daily routine to strengthen my overall confidence levels?

Notes

THE JOURNEY TO PURSUING PASSIONS

> *"Efforts and courage are not enough without purpose and direction,"* – **JFK**

Now that we have explored the transformative power of turning pain into power, it is essential to dig deeper into the concept of purpose. What does it mean to live a life driven by purpose and how can we align our actions and goals with a sense of direction and meaning? Let's shift our focus toward unraveling the essence of purpose and how it can shape our lives in profound ways.

Purpose

Have you ever watched a young woman speak her mind or seen a group of girls working diligently on their dance routines to make the team? These individuals are living out their purpose, whether they realize it or not. Purpose is not a fixed destination but an ongoing journey that shapes our actions and decisions. For many young women ages 15-25, finding their purpose can be a daunting task, especially in the face of adversity and obstacles.

It is essential to understand that purpose is not something to be discovered but something to be embraced daily. Adversity and obstacles can be powerful tools in helping us uncover our true purpose. Just like a diamond is formed under pressure, our purpose can shine brightest when we face challenges head-on. As young women navigating through life, it is crucial to recognize that your purpose is not defined by external expectations but by your inner drive and passion.

As you encounter trauma and challenges along the way, it is essential to remember that these experiences can shape your purpose and help you grow stronger.

Childhood trauma is a common occurrence that can have a lasting impact on our lives. According to The National Child Traumatic Stress Network, *"When children have been in situations where they feared for their lives, believed that they would be injured, witnessed violence, or tragically lost a loved one, they may show signs of child traumatic stress."* By acknowledging and understanding our past experiences, we can use them as fuel to propel us towards our purpose.

Discovering My Purpose in Healthcare

As a young girl, I witnessed the dedication and hard work of both my grandmothers, who immigrated from Jamaica to the United States and took on multiple jobs as nurses' aides to support their families. Their resilience and compassion inspired me and ignited my passion for healthcare. They became my role models, showing me the strength and determination of a powerful black woman. When my paternal grandmother succumbed to a rare form of brain cancer during my high school years, it was a traumatic moment that propelled me toward a healthcare career. I aspired to become a neurosurgeon, driven by a desire to find a cure for the disease that had taken my grandmother's life. However, a humorous realization about my aversion to math led me to reconsider my path.

Choosing to pursue nursing was a transformative decision that I have never regretted.

Nursing is the heartbeat of healthcare, and it is the most trusted profession in the country for a reason. Graduating from Binghamton University's Decker School of Nursing was a significant milestone that equipped me with the knowledge and skills necessary for a successful healthcare career. Over the past twenty-three years, I have worked as a Registered Nurse specializing in orthopedics, trauma, bariatrics, and neurosurgery before transitioning to outpatient neurology. My education and experiences at Binghamton not only prepared me for my nursing career but also laid the foundation for a future endeavor - the non-profit organization that I would later establish.

Life is unpredictable, and we may encounter pain, adversity, or challenges. It is how we navigate through these obstacles and emerge stronger that defines our character. In my journey through healthcare, I have learned that overcoming hardships and embracing challenges have shaped me into the nurse and individual I am today. My purpose in healthcare goes beyond treating patients; it is about making a difference, advocating for those in need, and providing compassionate care to those facing medical challenges. As I continue to grow in my profession, I am grateful for the opportunity to serve others and contribute to the well-being of my community.

How I Handled Adversity

Upon realizing my aversion to math, which posed a significant obstacle to my dream of becoming a neurosurgeon, I could have been discouraged and given up. However, I chose to approach the situation with resilience and determination. Instead of letting this setback define me, I took a step back to assess my strengths and interests. It was during this introspection that I discovered my true calling in nursing.

Opting to pursue a career in nursing ignited a newfound passion within me. The realization that so many patients, regardless of their diagnosis, rely on compassionate and skilled healthcare professionals resonated deeply with me. This passion for helping others and making a positive impact fuels my dedication to nursing today. Despite engaging in various endeavors, nursing remains at the forefront of my priorities because of the fulfillment it brings me.

In times of adversity, it is crucial not to lose sight of your purpose or passions. Instead of giving up when faced with challenges, it is essential to engage in self-reflection. By delving into what brings you happiness, whom you aspire to assist, and the unique value you wish to contribute, you can navigate through obstacles with resilience and determination. Remember, adversity may test your resolve, but it is through these moments of introspection and determination that you can emerge stronger and more aligned with your true purpose and passions.

My own experiences with adversity and trauma have shaped me into the person I am today. By acknowledging my pain and using it as a source of strength, I have positively impacted those around me. As young women, you have the power to turn your struggles into triumphs and use them to fuel your purpose.

In conclusion, the purpose is not a fixed destination but an ongoing journey that evolves as you grow and learn. By embracing adversity and obstacles, you can uncover your purpose and make a meaningful impact on the world around you. As a young woman, you have the power to shape your destiny and create a future filled with purpose and fulfillment.

Remember, your purpose is not defined by external expectations but by your inner drive and passion. Embrace the challenges that come your way, for they are opportunities for growth and self-discovery. Through determination and resilience, you can navigate through adversity and emerge stronger on the other side.

In my journey to purpose in healthcare, I have learned that setbacks can lead to unexpected opportunities. Embrace the journey, face challenges head-on, and let your purpose shine. Your unique contribution to the world awaits, and the obstacles you face today will only make you stronger tomorrow. Trust in your inner drive and passion and let them guide you as you navigate through life's challenges.

Self-Reflection

Reflect on the questions ahead and think about how the lessons learned and interests pursued in your past can lead you toward a future brimming with satisfaction and meaning.

1. What activities or interests bring you the most joy and fulfillment?
2. How have past challenges or obstacles shaped your perspective and strengths?
3. Who are your role models, and what qualities do you admire in them?
4. What unique talents or skills do you possess that can contribute to your purpose?
5. What causes or issues ignite a passion within you and drive you to act?

6. How do you respond to adversity and setbacks, and what have you learned from these experiences?

7. How do you define success and fulfillment for yourself?

8. What goals or aspirations do you have for your future, and how do they align with your values and passions?

9. How can you practice self-care and maintain a healthy balance while pursuing your purpose?

10. What steps can you take today to move closer to living a purpose-driven life, even in the face of adversity?

NOTES

# Love, Lift, Lead

CREATING SUCCESS

"The key to life is accepting challenges. Once someone stops doing this, he's dead." - **Bette Davis**

We have explored the importance of resilience in facing challenges and overcoming obstacles. It is essential to respond to challenges with determination and grit, especially for young girls and women who may be going through tough times.

Resilience is the ability to turn pain into power, and it begins with the core pillars of Love, Lead, and Lift. By practicing self-love, showing love to others, and using our leadership abilities to inspire and empower, we can make a lasting impact on the world around us.

To show up as our best selves, we must incorporate these principles into our lives. By rediscovering our identity and purpose through self-love, developing strategies to overcome challenges through leadership, and uplifting others to channel our pain into strength, we can thrive in the face of adversity.

Purpose is an ongoing journey that evolves with challenges and adversity, and it is driven by inner passion rather than external expectations. Embrace challenges, let purpose guide actions, and find fulfillment in pursuing passions.

Remember, you have the strength within you to overcome any obstacle. Embrace your resilience and know that you are powerful beyond measure. Let this book be your guide for facing challenges, offering practical steps to navigate tough times and emerge stronger by love, lifting others, and leading by example.

The world is waiting for you to shine. You can rise above adversity and show the world the power of resilience.

As stated earlier, confidence is the key to continuing to overcome adversity and achieving long-term success. By embracing resilience, practicing self-love, leading with purpose, and lifting others, you can confidently navigate challenges and emerge stronger than before. Remember, you have the strength within you to thrive in the face of any obstacle, rise above adversity, persevere, and show the world the power of resilience.

With Love,

Shantay Carter

NOTES

Empowerment Course Invitation

Are you ready to embark on a journey of self-discovery, empowerment, and personal growth together?

Thank you for taking the time to read this book. I hope that you found the principles and self-reflective questions helpful. If you are interested in receiving further guidance and coaching from our community to achieve long-term success, then I invite you to enroll in my new course - The Love, Lift, Lead Empowerment Course. This course is designed to help you embrace your past experiences, build confidence, and unlock your leadership potential with love and support.

What You'll Gain from the Course:

- Practical tools and strategies for overcoming adversity and embracing growth
- A community of support and encouragement from like-minded individuals
- Confidence-building techniques to boost your self-assurance and self-esteem
- Leadership development skills to help you lead with authenticity and purpose

Course Features:

- Interactive learning catering to high school and college girls
- Expert guidance from experienced mentors in the fields of personal development and empowerment
- Engaging activities, worksheets, and resources to apply the teachings of love, lift, and leadership in your daily life
- Ongoing support from a community of impactful people

Don't miss this opportunity to transform your life and unlock your full potential with expert guidance and a supportive community. Join us on this empowering journey and let love, lift, and leadership guide you towards a brighter and more fulfilling future. Send an e-mail to shantayc@hotmail.com to start your transformation with Love, Lift, Lead!

NOTES

About The Author

Shantay Carter, BSN, RN

Regarding Shantay Carter, helping others is more than a job, it's her passion and purpose, from her daily work as a dedicated nurse to her ambitions as the founder of a thriving nonprofit organization. The New York area native has an extensive history of letting her caring nature guide her path.

Shantay attended Binghamton University, receiving a Bachelor of Science degree in Nursing. In 2000, she began working at Binghamton General Hospital as a Registered Nurse. In 2002, Shantay continued her career at Northwell Health Systems as an orthopedic/ neurosurgery/ trauma nurse. In 2021, Shantay transitioned into outpatient care, where she currently works in a Neurology Multi-Specialty Practice for Summit Health.

After noticing the lack of guidance for young girls in the Long Island area, Shantay created Women of Integrity, Inc. The fourteen-year-old organization has already made considerable strides in its mission to *"empower and educate women of all ages and ethnicities."*

Shantay modestly holds several accomplishments and honors for her work. She's an award-winning empowerment leader and nurse. She is the best-selling author of Destined for Greatness. She is the Founder of Men of Integrity Inc. and Co-founder of Nurses Of Integrity. In 2021, Shantay was the Keynote Speaker for the ANA-NY 9th Annual Conference, and she was the Keynote Speaker for the 2022 North East Regional Conference of Chi Eta Phi Sorority, Incorporated. In 2023, Shantay had the honor of becoming a TEDx Speaker.

Shantay is a Proud Member of Alpha Kappa Alpha Sorority, Incorporated, the NAACP, The Nassau County Medical Reserve Corp., The American Nurses Association, The Greater NYC- Black Nurses Association, Chi Eta Phi Sorority, Incorporated, Sigma Theta Tau International Honor Society of Nursing, Board

Member for Author in a Box, and Member of the Hempstead Chamber of Commerce.

Shantay currently lives in Hempstead, NY, and when she's not helping patients or making teen girls feel amazing, you can find her enjoying music, art, baking…or flashing her award-winning smile.

Shantay's motto is:

"I believe that what you put out in life, you get back. So, if you put out positivity, then you will get back positivity— it's our job to give back in any way we can."

Author Contact Information:

Shantay Carter, BSN, RN

Website: https://linktr.ee/shantaycarter

Instagram: https://www.instagram.com/s.carterrn

Facebook: https://www.facebook.com/S.CarterRN/

NOTES

NOTES

NOTES

NOTES

NOTES

NOTES

NOTES

NOTES

NOTES

NOTES

NOTES

NOTES

NOTES

NOTES

Notes

NOTES

NOTES

NOTES

NOTES